P · O · C · K · E · T · S

HORSES

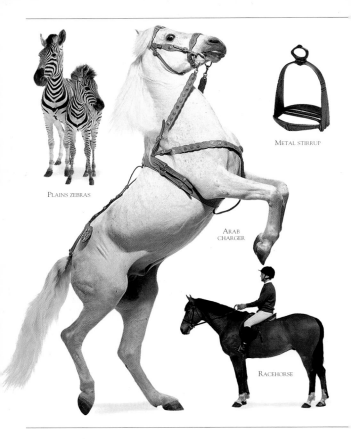

PLAINS ZEBRAS

METAL STIRRUP

ARAB
CHARGER

RACEHORSE

P·O·C·K·E·T·S

HORSES

Written by
DAVID ALDERTON

MOUNTED
POLICE OFFICER

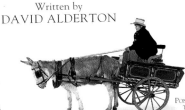

PONY AND
TRAP

SHIRE
HORSE

SHETLAND
PONY FOAL

DORLING KINDERSLEY
London • New York • Stuttgart

A DORLING KINDERSLEY BOOK

Project editor Alan Burrows
Art editor Carole Oliver
Senior editor Laura Buller
Senior art editor Helen Senior
Picture research Anna Lord
Production Louise Barratt

First published in Great Britain in 1995
by Dorling Kindersley Limited
9 Henrietta Street, Covent Garden, London WC2E 8PS

A CIP catalogue record for this book is available from
the British Library

ISBN 0 7513 5185 7

Colour reproduction by Colourscan, Singapore
Printed and bound in Italy by L.E.G.O.

CONTENTS

HOW TO USE THIS BOOK

These pages show you how to use *Pockets: Horses*. The book is divided into several sections. The main sections consist of information on different breeds of horse. There is also an introductory section at the front, and a reference section at the back. Each new section begins with a picture page, which gives an idea of what it is about.

HORSE TYPES

The horses in the book are arranged into four main types: ponies, light horses, heavy horses, and wild and feral horses. Each type features recognized breeds. Often, other breeds, which are considered as influences, are also included.

CORNER CODING

Corners of horse and pony pages are colour coded with yellow, blue, red, and green to remind you which section you are in.

- PONIES
- LIGHT HORSES
- HEAVY HORSES
- WILD AND FERAL HORSES

HEADING

This describes the subject of the page. This page is about the Cleveland Bay. If a subject continues over several pages, the same heading applies.

INTRODUCTION

This provides a clear, general overview of the subject, and gives key information that you need to know about it.

Corner coding

Heading

Introduction

LIGHT HORSES

CLEVELAND BAY

DESCENDED FROM the English Yorkshire Coach Horses of the 1800s, these versatile workers pull royal carriages on state occasions. The horses are called Cleveland Bays because they originally came from Cleveland on the north-eastern coast of England. They have a distinctive bay-coloured coat with a black mane and tail.

Muscular neck and sloping shoulders provide power

ROYAL CARRIAGE HORSES
The Cleveland Bays used in England to pull the royal carriages are kept in the Royal Mews near Buckingham Palace in London. At one time, the Duke of Edinburgh raced a team of part Cleveland Bays in driving competitions.

No feathering on the legs

94

Size indicator

CAPTIONS AND ANNOTATIONS

Each illustration has a caption. Annotations, in *italics*, point out features of an illustration.

RUNNING HEADS

These remind you which section you are in. The top of the left-hand page gives the section name. The top of the right-hand page gives the subject. This page comes from the section on light horses.

FACT BOXES

Many pages have fact boxes. These contain at-a-glance information about the horse featured on that page. This fact box gives interesting facts about the history of the Cleveland Bay.

Caption   *Running head*

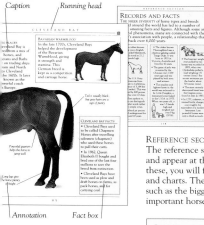

CLEVELAND BAY

BAVARIAN WARMBLOOD

In the late 1700s, Cleveland Bays helped the development of the Bavarian Warmblood, giving it strength and stamina. This German breed is kept as a competition and carriage horse.

Tail is usually black, but grey hairs are a sign of injury

CLEVELAND BAY FACTS

• Cleveland Bays used to be called Chapmen Horses after travelling salesmen (chapmen) who used these horses to pull their carts.

• In 1862, Queen Elizabeth II bought and bred one of the last four stallions to save the breed from extinction.

• Cleveland Bays have been used as plow and draft horses on farms, as pack horses, and for carrying coal.

Powerful quarters help the horse to jump well

Long legs give the horse plenty of speed

Annotation   *Fact box*

LABELS

For greater clarity, some pictures have labels. They may give extra information, or identify a picture when it is not obvious from the text what it is.

REFERENCE SECTION

The reference section pages are yellow and appear at the back of the book. On these, you will find useful facts, figures, and charts. These pages give horse records, such as the biggest and smallest, and important horse care information.

INDEX

You will find an index at the back of *Pockets: Horses*. This acts as a species and a subject index. All subjects and types of horse covered in the book are listed alphabetically.

INTRODUCTION
TO HORSES

WHAT IS A HORSE?

SOME 60 MILLION YEARS AGO the first horses ran on
the plains of North America. The modern horse has
four legs, each with a single toe, and has a coat of
short hair. Like all mammals, horses suckle their
young, and as herbivores, their natural
food is grass. They are
social creatures
and prefer to live
in groups.

*Long tail helps
to keep flies off
the body*

*The chest is deep
and wide to give
an adequate lung
capacity.*

*Powerful muscles in
the hindquarters
give the horse thrust
when running.*

*Hooves are made
of a protein called
keratin.*

HORSE FACTS

• Horses are measured
from the ground up to
the withers, which is
the highest point of the
shoulders.

• Unlike horses, pony
foals have the same
proportions as adults.

• There are about 60
officially registered
light horse breeds.

• Most modern horse
breeds have been
deliberately created to
do a specific task.

Long hair on the back of the neck is called a mane

Horses have an excellent sense of hearing.

Withers

Long head and neck allow horse to graze while standing

It takes four months for a horse foal to take on adult proportions.

Long legs developed to run from danger

HORSES AND HUMANS
As this cave painting shows, early humans hunted horses for their meat and skin. By keeping horses in herds, these essentials became more easily available. Eventually, horses were used for riding and pulling carts, and later were bred to do all kinds of work.

BORN TO RUN
Both wild and domestic horses give birth to fully developed offspring. This is because in the wild the young foal has to be able to keep up with its mother from birth to graze in fields and escape from predators.

THE HORSE IN HISTORY

AT FIRST, HUMANS SAW the horse as a source of meat for food, and skin for clothes. Domestication of horses began 5,000 to 6,000 years ago, originally to herd cattle and sheep, and later to pull carts and chariots. Soon, horses became the normal means of transport and travel, and were vital in warfare.

BEFORE HORSES
Oxen or onagers were domesticated before horses. A Mesopotamian mosaic of 2500 B.C. shows a team of onagers pulling a chariot.

CHARIOTS
After horse-riding tribes made contact with the Egyptians, horses and hinnies (the offspring of a male horse and a female donkey) became preferred as a means of transport in Egypt. Both animals are painted on this Egyptian tomb of c.1400 B.C.

Horse

Hinny

CONSTELLATION OF PEGASUS

MYTHOLOGICAL STORIES
According to ancient Greek mythology, the winged horse Pegasus rose from the blood of the Medusa and was caught by Athena, the goddess of wisdom, who tamed him with a golden bridle. Later, Greek astronomers gave the name Pegasus to a group of stars in the northern sky.

HUNTING FOR PLEASURE
Horses have been used for hunting for centuries. This mosaic is from late 5th- or 6th-century North Africa.

6TH-CENTURY PERSIAN PLATE

EMPIRE BUILDERS
In the 6th century, Persians used horses to create the first sizeable empire. The Persians were excellent riders and defeated their enemies with horse-drawn chariots and cavalry. They also built roads and set up an efficient postal system, relying on horses, to help them run their domain.

More horses in history

Before the arrival of the steam engine, just about everything was moved by horses. People travelled in carts and carriages, and goods went by pack horses on roads or by horse-drawn barges on canals. In war, the role of the horse changed from carrying knights into battle, to transporting guns and supplies. Horses were popular as children's toys, much in the same way as cars are today.

BARGE HORSES
The first canal barges in the 18th century were pulled by horses on a towpath beside water. Loads of up to 50 tonne (tons) were hauled at speeds about 3.3 km/h (2 mph).

JOUSTING
In 15th-century Europe, mounted knights prepared for war by jousting. In this sport, a knight tried to unhorse his opponent or break his own lance against the other's shield. A fully loaded jousting horse carried around 190 kg (419 lb) of knight, armour, and saddle.

Brightly coloured caparison covers horse

Leather gauntlet glove

Heavy chain mail armour

HISTORICAL FACTS
• El Cid, the Christian warrior, called his horse *Babieca*, the Spanish word for "stupid".

• A "freelance" was a medieval mercenary with a horse and lance.

• An Austrian horse-drawn railway opened in 1852; it was 200 km (124 miles) long.

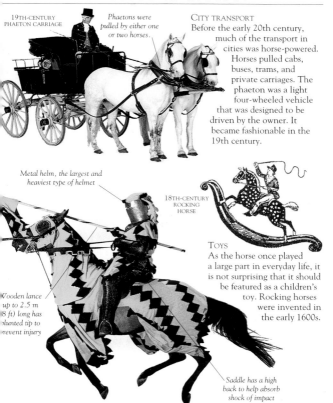

19TH-CENTURY PHAETON CARRIAGE

Phaetons were pulled by either one or two horses.

CITY TRANSPORT

Before the early 20th century, much of the transport in cities was horse-powered. Horses pulled cabs, buses, trams, and private carriages. The phaeton was a light four-wheeled vehicle that was designed to be driven by the owner. It became fashionable in the 19th century.

Metal helm, the largest and heaviest type of helmet

18TH-CENTURY ROCKING HORSE

TOYS

As the horse once played a large part in everyday life, it is not surprising that it should be featured as a children's toy. Rocking horses were invented in the early 1600s.

Wooden lance up to 2.5 m (8 ft) long has blunted tip to prevent injury

Saddle has a high back to help absorb shock of impact

THE FIRST HORSES

THE ORIGINS OF today's horses can be traced back over 60 million years. The first horses probably started to evolve in what is now the south-eastern part of North America, before the continents split and moved to their present positions. Horses became extinct there about 8,000 years ago, but thrived in Asia, Africa, and Europe.

HIPPARION
This was the last of the three-toed horses. Its remains have been found in Europe, Asia, and Africa, where it lived up to 15,000 years ago.

SKULL
Small teeth ideal for browsing

FOUR-TOED FOOT
Four toes on front feet good for marshy land

EOHIPPUS
This small browsing animal, no bigger than a hare, was the ancestor of the modern horse. It became extinct about 40 million years ago.

SKULL
Narrow jaw and longer head

THREE-TOED FOOT
Fewer toes better for running on hard ground

MESOHIPPUS
As the forests began to thin out, and the land became drier and harder, early horses such as Mesohippus could run and trot over long distances.

SKULL
Incisor teeth begin to develop

THREE-TOED FOOT
Outside toes are still prominent

MIOHIPPUS
This was a more advanced form of Mesohippus and lived around 30 million years ago. By now, its leg movement was similar to that of a modern horse.

ORIGINS

Land bridges helped horses to establish their present distributions. The Bering land bridge between North America and Asia was cut at the end of the last Ice Age because of the rising sea level. This separated the populations of horses.

Bering land bridge

60 MILLION YEARS AGO

PRESENT DAY

FIRST HORSE FACTS

• Scientists suspect that a disease wiped out the early North American horses.

• The first *Eohippus* was discovered in 1867 in Wyoming, U.S.A.

• The wild ancestral horses of South America are all extinct.

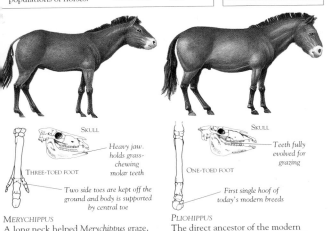

SKULL

Heavy jaw holds grass-chewing molar teeth

THREE-TOED FOOT

Two side toes are kept off the ground and body is supported by central toe

SKULL

Teeth fully evolved for grazing

ONE-TOED FOOT

First single hoof of today's modern breeds

MERYCHIPPUS

A long neck helped *Merychippus* graze, rather than browse. This horse lived on the prairies of present-day Nebraska, in the North American mid-west. about 10 million years ago.

PLIOHIPPUS

The direct ancestor of the modern horse, *Pliohippus* lived about six million years ago. It had the general proportions of today's equines and stood around 122 cm (48 in) high at the shoulder.

MAIN HORSE TYPES

MOST MODERN HORSES are thought to be descended from four types which inhabited Europe and Asia over 6,000 years ago. Their features can still be seen in some breeds today. Domestication led to the variety of modern breeds and their spread across the world.

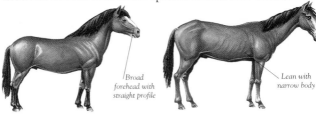

Broad forehead with straight profile

Lean with narrow body

Small head

PONY TYPE 1
This hardy pony looked similar to today's Exmoor breed of Great Britain. It lived in north-western Europe.

HORSE TYPE 1
Originating from central Asia, this horse lived in dry, arid conditions and resembled the modern Akhal-Teke.

PONY TYPE 2
Similar to Przewalski's horse, the Type 2 was powerfully built with a heavy head and roamed over northern Eurasia.

HORSE TYPE 2
Living in the hot deserts of western Asia, this slim horse was possibly the ancestor of the Arab and Caspian.

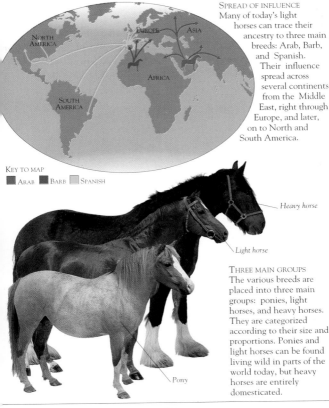

SPREAD OF INFLUENCE
Many of today's light
horses can trace their
ancestry to three main
breeds: Arab, Barb,
and Spanish.
Their influence
spread across
several continents
from the Middle
East, right through
Europe, and later,
on to North and
South America.

KEY TO MAP
🟥 ARAB 🟫 BARB 🟨 SPANISH

Heavy horse

Light horse

THREE MAIN GROUPS
The various breeds are
placed into three main
groups: ponies, light
horses, and heavy horses.
They are categorized
according to their size and
proportions. Ponies and
light horses can be found
living wild in parts of the
world today, but heavy
horses are entirely
domesticated.

Pony

BODY AND CONFORMATION

A HORSE'S BODY IS perfectly designed for its way of life. The neck is long so it can stoop to graze, and long, muscular legs allow it to run away from danger. The proportions of a horse's body, or conformation, are used to determine its group and breed.

Points

The external features of a horse are called the points. Each point has a different name and together they make up the horse's conformation.

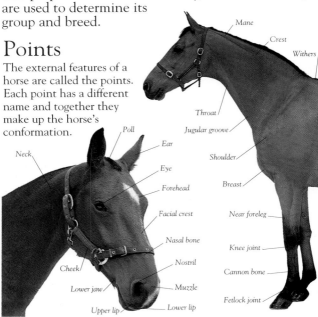

Mane

Crest

Withers

Throat

Jugular groove

Shoulder

Breast

Near foreleg

Knee joint

Cannon bone

Fetlock joint

Poll

Neck

Ear

Eye

Forehead

Facial crest

Nasal bone

Nostril

Cheek

Lower jaw

Muzzle

Upper lip

Lower lip

PROPORTION
In a perfectly
proportioned
horse, certain
measurements
of the body should
all be equal. Those
shown in blue should
correspond to each other,
as should the lines drawn
in both red and grey.

Head should be
same size as side
of blue squares

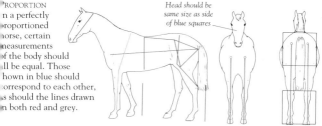

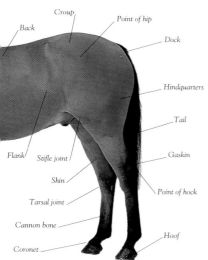

Croup

Back

Point of hip

Dock

Hindquarters

Tail

Flank

Stifle joint

Gaskin

Shin

Tarsal joint

Point of hock

Cannon bone

Hoof

Coronet

FRONT AND REAR LIMBS
When viewed from the
front, a line from the
shoulder should pass
through the centre of the
knees, fetlock, and foot. A
straight line should also
pass through the rear legs.

ANATOMICAL FACTS

• The body and head of
a horse are streamlined
and this helps to reduce
wind resistance.

• A long neck and
well-sloped shoulders
may indicate that the
horse is fast and good
for riding.

• Large eyes usually
show not only that the
horse has good vision,
but also a calm nature
and intelligence.

Skeleton and muscles

The framework of the horse consists of a skeleton, made up of a number of connected bones that are moved by muscles. Along the spinal, or vertebral, column, which runs from the head to the tail, is the spinal cord – the connection between the horse's brain and body. When a horse wants to move, it sends a message from its brain down the cord via nerves to signal the appropriate muscle.

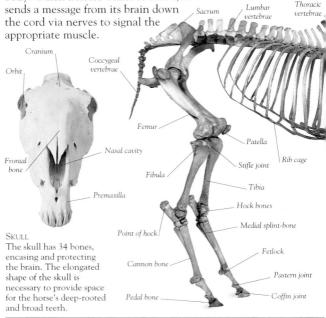

Lumbar vertebrae

Thoracic vertebrae

Sacrum

Cranium

Coccygeal vertebrae

Orbit

Femur

Patella

Nasal cavity

Rib cage

Frontal bone

Stifle joint

Fibula

Tibia

Premaxilla

Hock bones

Point of hock

Medial splint-bone

Cannon bone

Fetlock

Pastern joint

Pedal bone

Coffin joint

SKULL
The skull has 34 bones, encasing and protecting the brain. The elongated shape of the skull is necessary to provide space for the horse's deep-rooted and broad teeth.

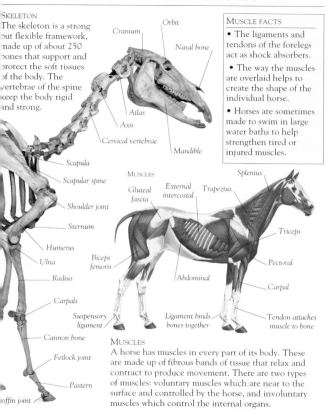

SKELETON

The skeleton is a strong but flexible framework, made up of about 250 bones that support and protect the soft tissues of the body. The vertebrae of the spine keep the body rigid and strong.

Orbit
Cranium
Nasal bone
Atlas
Axis
Cervical vertebrae
Mandible

Scapula
Scapular spine
Shoulder joint
Sternum
Humerus
Ulna
Radius
Carpals
Cannon bone
Fetlock joint
Pastern
Coffin joint

Biceps femoris
Suspensory ligament

MUSCLE FACTS

• The ligaments and tendons of the forelegs act as shock absorbers.

• The way the muscles are overlaid helps to create the shape of the individual horse.

• Horses are sometimes made to swim in large water baths to help strengthen tired or injured muscles.

MUSCLES

Gluteal fascia
External intercostal
Trapezius
Splenius
Triceps
Pectoral
Carpal
Abdominal
Ligament binds bones together
Tendon attaches muscle to bone

MUSCLES

A horse has muscles in every part of its body. These are made up of fibrous bands of tissue that relax and contract to produce movement. There are two types of muscles: voluntary muscles which are near to the surface and controlled by the horse, and involuntary muscles which control the internal organs.

COAT COLOURS

HORSES COME IN a variety of colours, patterns, and markings. Some breeds include horses of different colours, while others, such as the Palomino, are defined as breeds primarily by the colour of their body, mane, and tail, and certain distinguishing marks.

UNIQUE PATTERN
The zebra's striped pattern consists of black stripes on a white coat.

GREY
White and black hairs, over black skin.

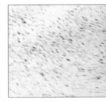

FLEABITTEN
Grey coat, flecked with brown specks of hair.

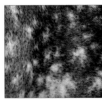

DAPPLE GREY
Grey base, with rings made of dark grey hairs.

PALOMINO
Gold, with white mane and tail; little black.

CHESTNUT
Golden, varying from pale to rich reddish gold.

LIVER CHESTNUT
Darkest possible shade of chestnut colouring.

BAY
...eddish brown to dark ...old, with black points.

BROWN
Black and brown, with black mane, tail, and legs.

BLACK
Solid black, sometimes with small white marks.

STRAWBERRY-ROAN
...hestnut body colour, ...ixed with white hairs.

BLUE ROAN
Black or brown coat hairs mixed with some white.

DUN
Either yellow, blue, or mouse-brown colour.

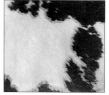

SPOTTED
...mall spots; sometimes ...lled appaloosa.

SKEWBALD
Base colour broken by large patches of white.

PIEBALD
Black and white patches in no fixed pattern.

Patterns and markings

One of the ways horse breeds are distinguished from each other is by marks on their body. These can be either natural or acquired. Natural markings are often areas of white hair on the head, legs, and hooves. Acquired markings are the result of branding or injury. Branding has been done for more than 2,000 years and can help to identify the horse if it is stolen.

FACE MARKINGS
While some breeds are defined by their coat patterns, face markings help to identify individual horses. The most common face markings are named below.

BLAZE

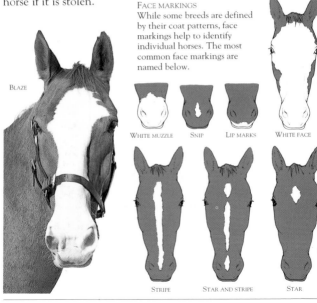

WHITE MUZZLE   SNIP   LIP MARKS   WHITE FACE

STRIPE   STAR AND STRIPE   STAR

ERMINE   SOCK   STOCKING   ZEBRA

LEG MARKINGS

These markings are often white. They are called ermine if they are just above the hoof, a sock if they cover the whole foot, and a stocking when extending above the knee. Zebra markings are dark rings.

HOOF MARKINGS

The blue hoof is made of hard blue horn and is most often associated with ponies. Hooves of black and white vertical stripes are seen on the Appaloosa and other spotted horse breeds.

BLUE HOOF   STRIPED HOOF

DORSAL STRIPE

This mark extends from the tail to the withers. It is found on primitive horses such as the Tarpan, and is associated with dun-coloured coats.

IDENTITY MARKINGS

Artificial markings help identify ownership and sometimes breed. Brand marks are applied by a hot iron rod which stops the hair growing back. Freeze marks are frozen on in a similar way.

BRAND MARK   FREEZE MARK

MOVEMENT

HORSES HAVE FOUR TYPES of movement, called paces.
These are the walk, trot, canter, and gallop. The walk
is the slowest pace. The horse can then accelerate to
a trot, going faster still when cantering. Running at
top speed is galloping. In every case, the hooves touch
down in a different sequence called a gait.

ACTION
To move forwards, a horse bends
its front legs at the knee and
extends the lower limb in front
of its body, placing each foot
on the ground in sequence.
This movement, known
as the action, varies
between breeds.

*A horse can walk at
about 8 km/h (3 mph)
and gallop up to
70 km/h (43 mph)*

*Slope of shoulders
directly influences
movement.*

*Horses can
change their
leading leg in
mid-gallop.*

WALKING
When a horse walks, it places its
four legs on the ground in regular
succession. The strides are of equal
distance and their length depends on
the size of the horse and its action.

JUMPING

The horse uses its hind-legs to power its leap forwards and upwards. As it jumps, it folds its legs under its body, then stretches down, touching the ground with one foreleg, immediately followed by the other.

Legs are folded under body to avoid obstacles.

GOOD MOVER
The Criollo from Argentina is often regarded as the most robust breed in the world. Descended from Spanish stock, it has powerful joints and good feet to assist its movement.

Horses will instinctively jump obstructions.

A foal can keep up with its mother within hours of its birth.

MOVEMENT FACTS

• Ponies pick their feet up high as they move, giving what is known as a high action.

• Light horses hardly bend their knees. This allows each stride to cover more ground.

• The straight angle of their shoulders allows heavy horses to bend their knees more than other horse types, to give a greater pull.

FOOD AND DIET

LIKE ANY ANIMAL, horses get their energy from food. They are herbivores, which means they do not eat meat. In the wild, horses can survive on grass and herbs as long as their grazing area is large enough. In the winter, when it is cold and there is less food, wild horses get out of condition, while in the summer they put on weight.

FIR
SOLID FO
Young horses a
able to eat their fi
solid food from abo
six week

*Waste expel
from rectu*

*Oesophagus
takes food to
stomach*

*Most digestion
takes place in the
large intestine*

*Teeth start
to grind
down food*

*Stomach holds
food*

*Colon absorbs
B vitamins*

Rib cage

*Small intestine
absorbs energy
from food*

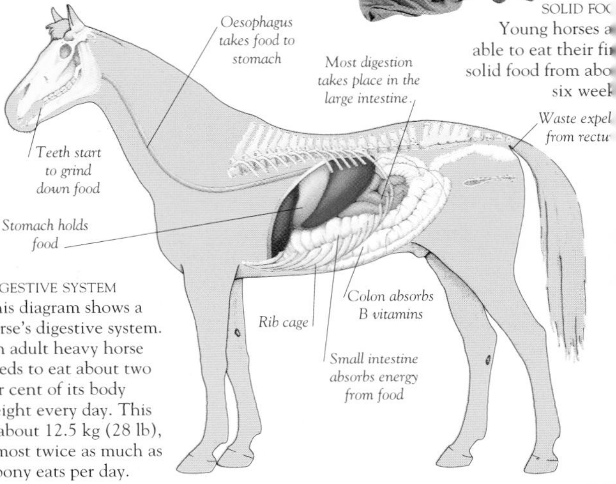

DIGESTIVE SYSTEM
This diagram shows a horse's digestive system. An adult heavy horse needs to eat about two per cent of its body weight every day. This is about 12.5 kg (28 lb), almost twice as much as a pony eats per day.

TEETH AND JAWS

Grazing wears down the foal's milk teeth and by the time the horse is five, these are replaced by a set of 40 adult teeth. The incisors cut the food into small pieces and the molars grind it down, ready for digestion.

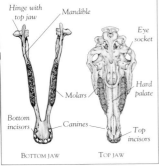

Hinge with top jaw

Mandible

Eye socket

Molars

Hard palate

Bottom incisors

Canines

Top incisors

BOTTOM JAW TOP JAW

BALANCED DIET

Horses need a balanced diet, with enough vitamins and minerals to help them stay healthy and in condition. Horses should be fed little and often. Water with the meal keeps the horse from becoming dehydrated.

Fruit and root vegetables must be chopped up lengthways so the horse does not choke.

Feed bowl holds carrots, maize, linseed, nuts, chaff, and a slice of apple

Hay is grass that has been cut and dried.

Bucket of clean, fresh water

FOOD DANGERS

• Plants like deadly nightshade, bracken, and ragwort may poison a horse if it eats even a small quantity. Pastures where horses are left to graze must be cleared of these plants.

• Horses should not graze in an area within 14 days of any spraying.

BEHAVIOUR

TODAY'S DOMESTIC HORSES show the same patterns of behaviour as their wild ancestors. The herd instinct still dominates, and horses prefer to be kept in groups rather than on their own. Much of their behaviour is linked to the way they communicate with other horses.

Horses sleep for only short periods at a time.

SLEEPING
Horses are able to sleep standing up. In the wild, this increases their chances of escaping from predators.

EARS
The position of a horse's ears is an important indicator of its mood. If the ears point forwards, this shows curiosity. When the horse is uncertain, it keeps one ear forwards and the other backwards.

SHIRE HORSE

FLEHMENING
When a mare is close to a stallion, the stallion may fold back his lips and draw air into his mouth, over its Jacobson's organ, to detect the mare's scent to sense if she is ready to mate. This action is called flehmening.

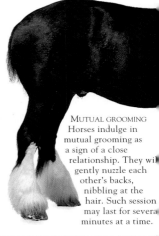

MUTUAL GROOMING
Horses indulge in mutual grooming as a sign of a close relationship. They will gently nuzzle each other's backs, nibbling at the hair. Such session may last for severa minutes at a time.

REARING
A stallion rears
up to intimidate
a rival, often
lashing out
with his front
feet at the
same time.

*Horse uses its
front legs to
balance*

*Horses
often rear
in play.*

ROLLING OVER
By rolling, a horse can exercise the
muscles in its back, and also clean its
coat. Horses often roll when turned
out to graze in
a field.

*Stallions rear
naturally
in the wild.*

*Horses nuzzle
each other to
establish their
relationship.*

SHETLAND
PONY

BEHAVIOURAL FACTS
• Horses will call out
to warn others of
approaching danger.
• The tail is used as a
fly swish rather than
for communication.
• Repeated pawing at
the ground with the
hooves is often a sign
of nervousness.
• A horse's ears are
very mobile and can
rotate independently
in a full circle.

LIFE CYCLE OF A HORSE

MARES NEED ONLY BE three or four years old before they are ready to give birth. After mating, it is almost a year before the foal is born and it takes another five before it becomes a fully grown adult horse. Most horses have a lifespan of around 25 years.

Early development

A mare is ready to mate at intervals of roughly three weeks from spring to autumn. During these intervals, which last four to six days, she is said to be on heat and will be ready to accept an approach by a stallion.

MATING
When a mare is on heat, her behaviour changes and she often seeks the company of other horses more than is usual.

Stallions have to be careful when they approach mares as the mare may kick out.

DEVELOPMENT FACTS
- Male foals usually spend more time in the womb than females.
- It is not obvious that a mare is pregnant until after five months.
- The mare's belly drops before she is ready to give birth.
- Mares can give birth after two years, but this is unusual.
- It is rare for a horse to give birth to twins.

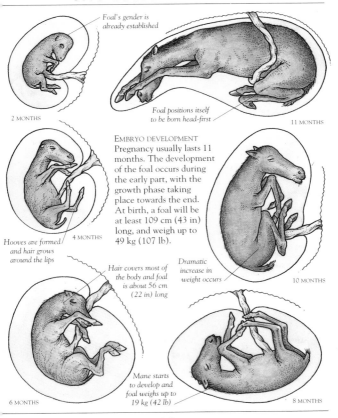

Foal's gender is
already established

2 MONTHS

Foal positions itself
to be born head-first

11 MONTHS

EMBRYO DEVELOPMENT
Pregnancy usually lasts 11
months. The development
of the foal occurs during
the early part, with the
growth phase taking
place towards the end.
At birth, a foal will be
at least 109 cm (43 in)
long, and weigh up to
49 kg (107 lb).

Hooves are formed
and hair grows
around the lips

4 MONTHS

Dramatic
increase in
weight occurs

10 MONTHS

Hair covers most of
the body and foal
is about 56 cm
(22 in) long

6 MONTHS

Mane starts
to develop and
foal weighs up to
19 kg (42 lb)

8 MONTHS

Growing up

The usual time for a foal to be born is
during early summer when grass and
other food is most plentiful, to help the
mare's milk supply. Horses develop
quickly from young foals into adults.
A horse can be independent of its
mother by the time it is six months
old and reach full adult size between
the ages of four and five years. It is at its
strongest between the ages of five and 15.

Mare licks foal clean

1 NEWBORN
A new foal can stand
on its feet within half an
hour of its birth. It is
carefully watched over
by its mother.

Foals take milk at frequent intervals

Legs are long in proportion to the body

2 TWO WEEKS
After two weeks, the foal is used to
walking. To give it extra stability, it
stands with its rear legs slightly apart as it
cannot yet straighten its legs. The hooves
are small and soft. The tail is short and
bushy, while the mane stands up on its
neck and is light and feathery.

Large eyes

3 FIVE WEEKS
At five
weeks, the foal
still has a soft
woolly coat,
known as
milk hair. As the upper
bones of its legs
become longer,
the foal can now
stand upright.

4 EIGHT WEEKS

The foal lives solely on its mother's milk for its first two months, after which it gradually begins to eat grass until it is fully weaned at around six months old. After two months, the foal's fluffy milk hair begins to be shed and is replaced by its adult coat.

Hindquarters become noticeably more muscular

Digestion changes during weaning

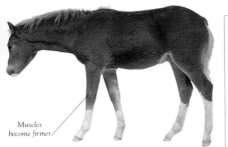

Muscles become firmer

5 FOUR MONTHS

The foal's body has grown to adult proportions. The neck and tail have lengthened and the limbs continue to become stronger as their muscles develop further. The hooves also become harder.

GROWING UP FACTS

• As soon as they are born, new foals shiver to maintain their body temperature.

• The mother's first milk, called colostrum, contains antibodies which protect the foal against infections.

• After weaning, horse breeders usually give foals a concentrated feed with supplements to ensure the foals grow to be healthy.

USES OF THE HORSE

IN SPITE OF THE SPREAD of mechanization, the horse still has a place in society. Today, horses can be found hard at work in cities, forests, and farmland. While traditional horse sports like racing and steeple-chasing remain popular, they are now being joined by leisure activities like trekking.

Working horses

Horses work in forests because they cause less damage than tractors. Farmers in developing countries also find horses easy to keep as they can live off the land. Though no longer used in war, horses are retained in many countries for ceremonial duties and the police horse has so far proved to be irreplaceable.

MULE TRAINS
Even in the late 20th century, it has been hard to find anything to replace the mule to transport goods over uneven ground. Mules are still used in India, China, and Southeast Asia.

London police horses undergo about 40 weeks of training.

40

CEREMONIAL DUTIES
Many countries still use horses for ceremonial duties. This dates from wars where horses were used as cavalry and to haul artillery.

POLICE HORSES
Mounted police can be seen in many cities today. Horses offer the rider a good view and mobility, and can move through crowds more easily than either motorcycles or cars.

WORKING HORSE FACTS
• More horses are bred in the United States for leisure riding than for herding cattle.

• India employs more mounted police than any other country in the world.

• Heavy horses are used in Canadian forests to pull up trees and take them away, and to cultivate the soil afterwards.

Working cow ponies in the U.S.A. tend to average 15 hh.

Average working life of a police horse is about 14 years.

BRITISH POLICE HORSES AND RIDERS IN CEREMONIAL DRESS

QUARTER HORSE

HERDING CATTLE
People first used the horse to herd sheep and cattle over 6,000 years ago and still do so in North America and Australia.

Horses for sport and leisure

Since the end of World War II, there has been a tremendous increase in the use of the horse for pleasure. Sports such as horse racing remain as popular as ever, and interest in horse events like show jumping and dressage has been heightened by television. Riding holidays are now a popular and relaxing pastime for many people.

POLO
Originating in China, polo was played at least 2,500 years ago by teams of up to 1,000 players. Today, two teams of four try to knock a ball into a goal with a long mallet.

Rider's actions are well controlled

DRESSAGE
A dressage test lasts about five minutes and shows the rider's control and the training of the horse. The sport has wide appeal and competitions are held at every level.

A hard hat protects the rider's head in case of a fall.

Rider sits on the horse's centre of balance.

Pony will cover 4.8–6.4 km (3–4 miles) in an hour

More experienced horse and rider leads trekking party

RACEHORSES

Horse racing has become a huge international industry. This statue in the Kentucky Horse Park, U.S.A., is of the famous racehorse Man O' War, or Big Red, who was beaten only once in 21 races. When he died in 1947, more than 1,000 people attended his funeral.

HORSE SPORTS FACTS

• The longest-running horse race is the Palio in Siena, Italy, begun in the 1200s and still run today. The winning horse attends a special banquet afterwards.

• The word polo comes from the Tibetan *pulu*, meaning ball.

• The first steeplechase was held in 1830 at St. Albans, England.

Riders learn to use aids such as the reins.

Each rider keeps a pony-length away from the next.

A novice rider is given a well-trained horse.

Many ponies are bred specifically for riding schools.

RIDING HOLIDAYS

Those who want to ride occasionally or just for pleasure, can take a riding holiday. These treks can last a single day or a whole week and demand little skill. The distance covered in each day varies between 40–80 km (25–50 miles). Trips are often supervised and provide an opportunity to reach beautiful and inaccessible areas of a country.

HORSE RIDING

PEOPLE HAVE RIDDEN HORSES for many different reasons. Even before the invention of the wheel, horses provided a fast means of transport. Soldiers rode horses during wartime and explorers often travelled on horseback over unknown territory.

Riding styles

Each riding style evolved with a specific purpose in mind. Spanish riding sought to preserve techniques learned by the medieval knights, and the more practical aspects of this style are still used by cattle workers. (The side-saddle is purely for elegance.)

High saddle provides security

Kimblewick Pelham bit must be used gently

Flat metal stirrup

SPANISH RIDING
The aim of the Spanish style is to improve the horse's balance and physique and to achieve complete harmony between the horse and rider. This style is the forerunner of modern dressage.

WESTERN RIDING

This style was derived from the Spanish settlers and adapted by U.S. cowboys who virtually lived in the saddle. The Western style allows the rider to sit deeper in the saddle and so have a less tiring ride.

Both reins are held in one hand

Apron has a heavy hem to stop it flying about

SIDE-SADDLE

Sometimes called the "Saddle of Queens", side-saddle riding was first seen over 600 years ago in the courts of Europe. It was soon considered un-ladylike to ride astride.

LIPIZZANER WITH SIDE-SADDLE RIDER

CLASSICAL RIDING SCHOOL

Riding as a trained skill was first made popular in Italy in the 16th century.

RIDING STYLE FACTS

• Until the end of the 14th century, most women rode astride.

• In classical riding, the horse's leaps or kicks above the ground are called airs.

• Spanish riding is from a military style.

Equipment

In the early days, horses were ridden either bareback or with a simple cloth pad and were guided by a rope attached to their lower jaw. It was only during the late Roman period that saddles were used for the first time. Stirrups were invented by the Chinese in the 5th century, but not seen in Europe until the 700s.

Rowel pricks the horse's side

BRASS ROWEL SPUR FROM SOUTH AMERICA, c.1800

Buckle attaches spur to boot

MOTIVATION
Spurs are used to urge a horse to go forward. In the past, some particularly cruel spurs were devised which cut into the horse's side, but today they seldom have sharp edges.

BIT
The rider controls the horse's movement by means of a bit. This small metal bar fits into the horse's mouth and is attached to the reins.

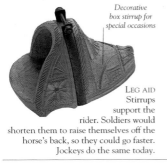

Decorative box stirrup for special occasions

LEG AID
Stirrups support the rider. Soldiers would shorten them to raise themselves off the horse's back, so they could go faster. Jockeys do the same today.

SADDLE
The saddle keeps the rider's weight off the horse's spine so its movement is not restricted. Custom-made saddles are now preferred to the older universal type.

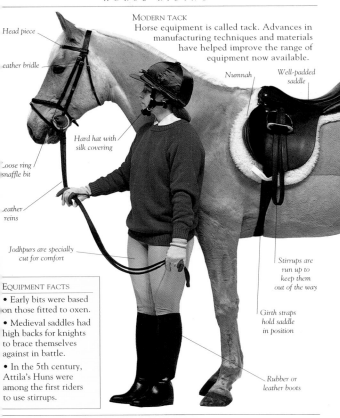

MODERN TACK

Horse equipment is called tack. Advances in manufacturing techniques and materials have helped improve the range of equipment now available.

Head piece

Leather bridle

Numnah

Well-padded saddle

Hard hat with silk covering

Loose ring snaffle bit

Leather reins

Jodhpurs are specially cut for comfort

Stirrups are run up to keep them out of the way

Girth straps hold saddle in position

Rubber or leather boots

EQUIPMENT FACTS

• Early bits were based on those fitted to oxen.

• Medieval saddles had high backs for knights to brace themselves against in battle.

• In the 5th century, Attila's Huns were among the first riders to use stirrups.

PONIES

INTRODUCTION TO PONIES

PONIES HAVE BEEN AROUND for thousands of years. Although ponies are closely related to the earliest horses, several characteristics distinguish them from today's breeds. Ponies are smaller, no taller than 14.2 hands high, with shorter legs in relation to their height. They also live longer and are hardier.

WARRIOR BREED
Despite their small size, ponies were used as war horses by European warriors such as Vikings

PONY POWER
In the past, ponies provided a means of transportation. Stronger for their size than horses, ponies were able to pull traps (small carts) without difficulty. Ponies are now popular for use in driving competitions.

Thick tail keeps out the cold

Wooden spoked wheels

19TH-CENTURY
IRISH TRAP

Head is similar to a Thoroughbred's

Strong hind-quarters

Limbs and joints must be strong and flexible

PONY FACTS

• The word pony comes from the French word *poulenet*, which is a small male horse.

• Ponies were first used down coal mines in the 1600s, hauling wagons of coal from the pit face to the surface.

• Robert the Bruce of Scotland defeated an English army in 1314, using light cavalry mounted on ponies.

POLO PONY

This is not a breed, but a type of pony produced for a particular purpose. Polo demands that the animal must be fast and sure-footed. So, the first Polo ponies were bred from a cross between Thoroughbreds for speed, and ponies for stability.

Short, powerful limbs with strong bones

Hard feet, which are rarely shod

HARD HOOF

Ponies are more sure-footed than horses. They have particularly tough hooves and seldom go lame. This is because the early breeds had to survive on the cold, damp moorlands of northern Europe.

SHETLAND

THESE PONIES WERE named after the bleak Shetland Islands off the north-east coast of Scotland, where they have been bred for more than 2,000 years. Their ancestors were either brought over from the mainland or from Scandinavia. In spite of their small size, the Shetlands are a tough and hardy breed.

Weather-resistant coat, double-layered in winter

LARGE AND SMALL
As more people have kept Shetlands, some breeders have developed a smaller pony for use as a pet. This has given rise to the Miniature Shetland which has proved popular.

Muscular neck

NATIVE HABITAT
There are no trees on the Shetland Islands to provide firewood, so islanders dug up peat on the moors for fuel. This was carried to their villages by the ponies, which are very strong for their small size.

Strong, rounded feet

10

This modern breed is the result of combining the Shetland primarily with Hackney blood, and bears no close resemblance to its island ancestor. The American pony is slimmer and has a more refined look.

Hair of mane and tail is long and thick

THELWELL CARTOON
The Shetland is a good choice for a young rider, but it can get fat if not exercised regularly – as this drawing by the British cartoonist Thelwell shows.

RIDING PONY
The Shetland is popular throughout the world as a riding pony. Its hock and knee joints are very supple and bend easily. This spring in its step helps it to walk safely on rocky, uneven ground, and avoid injury to its feet as it walks.

Long-haired tail, especially full to protect against the weather

Back legs are strong and firm

HIGHLAND

THE LARGEST AND STRONGEST of Britain's ponies is the Highland. Originally small, the size and strength of these ponies was increased by crossings with Percheron heavy horses in the 16th century. Later, Arab input made them more suitable for riding. Today's Highland combines strength with an easy-going nature.

Wide forehead combined with short head

Neck is long and strongly arched

Broad, wide nostrils

Strong forelegs with large flat knees

Long hair is soft and silky

CAVE DRAWINGS
This drawing from cave walls at Lascaux, France, dates back about 14,000 years to the end of the last Ice Age. The drawings show ponies similar to today's Highland breed and it may be that the ancestors of the Highland came from this part of Europe.

Pony reckoned to be about 13 hh

Western Isles

SCOTLAND

IRELAND   ENGLAND

HIGHLAND HOMELAND
Ponies have lived in the
upland areas of northern
Scotland and on some of
the nearby Western Isles
for more than 10,000
years. They are still used
in the forest, for
trekking, and in harness.

HIGHLAND FACTS

• In the circus ring, a
Highland has carried
seven adults on its
back, weighing a total
of 380 kg (840 lb).

• Many ponies have
dark "eel" stripes
running along the back
and down the tail.

• Highland ponies
were ridden in the
Jacobite uprisings in
Scotland during the
18th century.

COLOURED COATS
Highlands are bred in many colours. This pony is
dun with a black mane and tail, and black lower
legs. A dense double-layered coat gives good
protection in bad weather conditions.

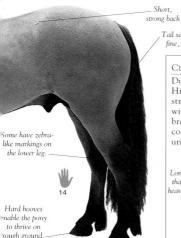

Short,
strong back

Tail set high and has
fine, silky texture

Some have zebra-
like markings on
the lower leg.

14

Hard hooves
enable the pony
to thrive on
rough ground.

CLYDESDALE INFLUENCE

During the 19th century, the
Highland was made bigger and
stronger as a result of crossings
with the Clydesdale. But the
breed's coarser looks were
considered to be
unattractive.

Longer legs
than most
heavy breeds

FELL AND DALES

THESE TWO MOORLAND BREEDS descend from Friesian horses, taken to Britain from Europe by the Romans to help with the building of Hadrian's Wall. This was built on the border between England and Scotland to keep out northern invaders and was completed in A.D. 120. Today, the sure-footedness of these two breeds has made them a popular choice for trekking.

Long tail trails close to the ground

Flexible joints lift feet clear of obstacles

14

TOUGH UPBRINGING

The natural habitat of the Fell and Dales is the rugged, hilly Pennine region of northern England. The Fell developed on the west side and the Dales on the east. The rough countryside has made both ponies hardy breeds, with plenty of stamina. They have hard feet, which do not wear down even when walking long distances over rough tracks. The ponies trot quickly and move freely.

FELL
The Fell is smaller and lighter than the Dales and was once preferred for riding. However, it could also carry heavy loads of 102 kg (224 lb) or more. It was not unusual for a pony to cover 384 km (240 miles) a week.

HACKNEY PONY

As a result of a bloodline developed in the 1880s, which was later cross-bred with Trotters and Roadsters, the Fell has added to the ancestry of the Hackney Pony.

Pony pulled traps during the 19th century

DALES

In the past, the heavier-built Dales were valued as pack ponies. They carried lead ore mined on the moors to the ports of north-eastern England.

Broad, open nostrils

Strong hindquarters

Firm, sloping shoulders

Tough blue horn hooves, with hair at the heels

14.2

Deep girth, with long and rounded ribs

EXMOOR AND DARTMOOR

NAMED AFTER THEIR moorland
habitats, both these ponies come
from south-western England. The
Exmoor is the oldest British breed
of pony and its ancestors may have
roamed over Exmoor before the
Bronze Age, about 4,000 years ago.
The younger Dartmoor dates back
1,000 years, but today's pony looks
little like it
did then.

WORKING PONY
Like most ponies, the
Exmoor and Dartmoor
have been used as pack
animals. The Dartmoor
used to carry tin from
mines on the moor to
nearby towns.

*Mottled colouring
on muzzle and
around the eyes*

EXMOOR PONY
Exmoor winters can be
harsh and these ponies
have had to adapt to
survive. A fan-like area
of hair at the top of their
tail prevents water from
penetrating and then
freezing. Large nostrils
warm the cold air as it is
breathed in.

*Compact body
with long ribs
and deep chest*

*Thick, springy
coat provides
warmth in winter*

*Short legs and
neat hooves*

12

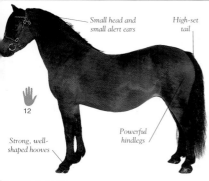

Small head and small alert ears

High-set tail

12

Strong, well-shaped hooves

Powerful hindlegs

EXMOOR PONY FACTS

• The eyes of the Exmoor pony are called "toad eyes", and are hooded to protect them from the rain and snow.

• The ponies dislike dogs, possibly because of an ancestral fear of wolves which used to live on Exmoor.

• Pure-bred Exmoors are marked with a star-shaped brand on their left shoulder, with their herd number beneath.

DARTMOOR PONY

As a result of crossings with other breeds, the modern Dartmoor is a particularly elegant-looking pony. It does not lift its knees as high as other ponies, making it less bouncy to sit on and so more comfortable to ride.

HARSH HABITAT

Dartmoor, in the English county of Devon, is crossed by the Dart, Tavy, and Taw rivers. Conditions here can be tough, and the ponies had to be hardy and sure-footed to thrive. Today, few of these ponies are still to be seen on the moors.

NEW FOREST PONY

FOR MORE THAN a thousand years, these hardy little ponies have roamed the New Forest in southern England. Oddly, the "forest" is mainly a large expanse of moorland covered with heather. Ponies have only been allowed to stay in the forest the whole year round since 1877. Until then, it was thought that there was not enough food for them. Even today, the herd is limited to 2,500 to prevent over-grazing.

Large head reflects the influence of other horse breeds

NEW FOREST FACTS

• The New Forest Pony is the second largest of the British Mountain and Moorland ponies.

• The ponies feed on prickly shrubs in winter. In spring, they must be watched closely to stop them wandering into boggy ground, where the first shoots of grass appear.

• Speeding vehicles injure or kill about 150 ponies every year.

NEW FOREST GUARDIANS

The ponies are owned by Commoners – people who have the right to graze their stock inside the forest. Four wardens, called Agisters, organize a round-up of the animals in late summer to check for any health problems and deal with any emergencies.

PONY AUCTION
Each year some of the
ponies are sold by
auction. Their friendly
nature means they are in
great demand for
young riders and
for driving.

Can be any
colour
except pinto
or albino

Straight,
powerful legs
and hard,
round hooves

IMPROVING THE BREED
The New Forest Ponies
have been pure-bred for
only 50 years. Many
breeds have played a part
in their history. Once, an
Arab stallion called
Zorah, owned by Queen
Victoria, was released into
the forest in an attempt to
breed with the ponies and
improve their appearance.

13

61

WELSH MOUNTAIN PONY AND AUSTRALIAN PONY

PONIES CAN BE related to each other, even if they live on opposite sides of the world. The Welsh Mountain Pony is the smallest and oldest of four Welsh breeds. In the early 19th century, many Welsh ponies were exported to Australia, where they played an important part in the development of the Australian Pony.

Large eyes

Wide nostrils

WELSH MOUNTAIN PONY
In the 18th century, the breed was influenced by a Thoroughbred called Merlin. In Wales, a pony is still called a "merlin".

PONIES OF THE VALLEY
Welsh Mountain Ponies still roam the Welsh valleys in some numbers.

Short, stocky body with a deep chest

Hooves are made of blue horn which is sound and hard.

13

USTRALIAN PONY
his breed still has a strong resemblance to its
'elsh relative and can be any solid colour. It is
ghly valued as a riding pony in Australia
here horse sports are very popular.

Narrow head with
long, crested neck
shows Arab ancestry

13

Body shape was
established by the
late 1920s.

Sloping shoulders give the
ponies a long stride and
smooth movements

VARIED MIXTURE
The early settlers of
Australia brought a
variety of breeds with
them and the Australian
Pony was developed
from these.

WELSH PONY FACTS

• Welsh Mountain
Ponies have many
attractive features,
including small,
pointed ears, and a
friendly face.

• The earliest records
of these ponies date
back to Roman times.

• Most of the ponies
are grey, but some are
bay, chestnut, or
palomino.

• The ponies eat
sparse, reedy grasses,
and mosses.

CONNEMARA

THE ONLY NATIVE Irish pony is the
Connemara. Its ancestors looked
like the Shetland and were ridden
across Europe by Celtic warriors
and traders. In the 16th century,
these ponies were mixed with the
Barb and Andalucians brought to
Ireland by Spanish merchants.
The result was the Irish Hobby,
a forerunner of the Connemara
which is used for riding,
dressage, and jumping.

ATLANTIC
OCEAN

IRELAND

GREAT
BRITAIN

Connemara

CONNEMARA COUNTRY
The pony is named after
the area of Connemara,
which is part of County
Galway, on the north-
western coast of Ireland

CONNEMARA FACTS

• Connemaras have
a particularly long
breeding life. Mares can
give birth until they are
33 years old.

• The first registered
Connemara stallion,
Cannon Ball, won the
annual farmers' race at
Oughterard, Ireland, for
16 successive years.

• In Galway, this pony
was used on farms and
as a pack animal to
carry seaweed, potatoes,
peat, and corn.

*Long tail is
set high*

*Length from
hips to the hocks
helps provide
thrust when
jumping*

*Long, strong
legs are good
for running*

*Grey is now the
most common
colour, though
palomino and
dun were once
familiar.*

FOOD AND SIZE
On the boggy ground of
their Irish homeland,
Connemaras exist on a
diet of sparse grass.
When given richer food,
they usually grow to a
larger size. Some larger
ponies are crossed with
Thoroughbreds to
produce racehorses.

WELSH COB INFLUENCE

In the 19th century, many Irish
farmers were very poor
and as a result, the
Connemaras also
suffered. Welsh Cobs
from Britain were
introduced to make
them stronger.

*Small, neat head shows
Arab influence*

HOMELAND HABITAT
The native environment of the
Connemara is a wild, isolated
expanse of marshes, lakes, and
mountains. The ponies have
been working on farms in this
area for centuries.

*Long neck
and sloping
shoulders show
the pony is good
for riding*

14

CHINCOTEAGUE

A BOOK AND A FILM have made this delightful little pony part of the childhood of many Americans. The Chincoteague lives on two islands off the eastern coast of the U.S.A. It is said to be descended from horses which survived a shipwreck close to the coast and swam ashore.

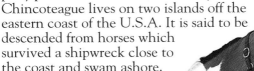

Large head compared to the rest of the body

Heavy shoulders and straight forelimbs

HORSE-LIKE PONY
It is likely that Spanish blood was originally involved in the ancestry of the Chincoteague, but poor grazing and possibly in-breeding have resulted in a reduction in its size. As a result, it resembles a small horse rather than a pony.

Legs are long, but joints may be poorly developed

12

Condition of the feet may vary

ISLAND HOME
The current population of around 200 Chincoteagues lives mostly on the island of Assateague, now a national park. The ponies are rounded up at the end of July for the annual sale, and made to swim across the channel to Chincoteague. Any ponies that are not sold return by the same route the following day.

CHINCOTEAGUE ISLANDS
Both Chincoteague and Assateague islands lie off the eastern coast of the state of Virginia in the U.S.A. Assateague was formed by a violent storm in 1933, which separated it from the mainland.

Dark brown coat

Thick coat provides good protection during the winter

COLOUR VARIATIONS
Chincoteagues come in different colours: piebald, skewbald, or more rarely pinto. Their coats tend to be slightly shaggy with a long mane and short tail.

HAFLINGER

THIS AUSTRIAN pony originates from the village of
Hafling in the Etschlander Mountains. It is descended
from other local ponies, the Arab, and extinct Alpine
Heavy Horse breeds. A true Haflinger is either
palomino or chestnut in colour, with a
flaxen mane and tail. It may be
harnessed or ridden.

*Flowing
flaxen tail is
thick and full*

*Noriker's
ancestors
were bred by
the Romans*

*Broad and
compact body with
a deep girth.*

HAFLINGER FACTS

• The young foals are
brought up on the
Alpine fields, where
their lungs develop in
the thin air.

• Haflingers are not
worked until they are
four years old.

• They may live for
more than 40 years.

NORIKER

Half of all horses in
Austria are Norikers.
The ancestors of this
native Austrian breed
were bred by the Romans
for draft and pack work.
Today, it is still a working
horse and can be seen
near the central Alpine
region, adjacent to the
Austrian Tyrol, home of
the Haflinger.

FLOWER BRAND
The Haflinger is also called the Edelweiss Pony because its brand is the shape of Austria's national flower.

EDELWEISS BRAND

Striking mane and small, elegant head, reflect Arab blood

Large eyes

Big nostrils

13

HAFLINGER
This pony is powerfully built, with well-made legs and sloping shoulders. The long back reflects its use as a pack pony. The ponies are sure-footed with a long stride, even when walking across steep mountainous terrain.

IN THE MOUNTAINS
In their native Austria, Haflingers are harnessed to sleighs as a means of transport in thick snow. Many are kept for use in the tourist season, when they pull old-fashioned carriages.

CASPIAN

THOUGHT TO HAVE BEEN EXTINCT for more than a thousand years, the Caspian was rediscovered in Iran in 1965. A small herd was established, but after wolves killed three mares and a foal, eight Caspians were sent to Britain where the breed has survived.

A Caspian has one more tooth than other horses.

CASPIAN FACTS

• The breed was rediscovered in 1965 by an American traveller, Louise L. Firouz.

• Twenty Caspians found in 1970 were used to start the Nourouzabad stud near Teheran, Iran.

• In Iran, the breed is known as both Ponseki and Monleki.

MINIATURE HORSE
The Caspian is usually described as a miniature horse rather than a pony. It has a short head, covered with the fine, thin skin of desert breeds, and large eyes and nostrils. The ears are very short and should not exceed 11 cm (4½ in).

Shoulders slope like a horse's, giving a longer stride than true ponies

11

Strong, oval-shaped feet never need shoeing

70

CASPIAN
SEA

Caspians
found in
this area

IRAN

AREA OF DISCOVERY
The pony is named after
the Caspian Sea, on the
border of Iran.

DESERT HABITAT
Caspians live in a remote part of Iran where there is
little rain and the temperature can vary widely. The
area is cut off from the rest of the country by the
Elburz mountains. This meant that the ponies did
not mix with other breeds and remained pure.

EGYPTIAN
CARVING

*Tail is
carried
high,
as on the
Arab*

CASPIAN ANCESTOR
The ancestor of the Caspian is thought to be the
smallest of the four main types of horse from which
all the main horse breeds developed. This type,
simply called Horse Type 4, lived in western Asia
and was probably no more than 9 hh. Miniature
horses similar to the Caspian have been found on
Eygptian artefacts 3,500 years old.

FALABELLA

THE SMALLEST BREED of horse in the world, the
Falabella is named after the Argentine family who
developed it. Although its size suggests it is a pony, its
proportions make it closer to a small horse. The
Falabella is generally kept as a pet, being unsuitable
for all but the very youngest rider. These little horses
may also be seen in the show ring, often
pulling scaled-down carts.

Long flowing and
luxurious tail

Long, silky
coat

Head should be
in proportion to
the body

Straight
shoulders

Appaloosa
colouring

A POPULAR CHOICE
The friendly nature of the
Falabella has meant that it is
kept the whole world over,
especially in North America.
Though expensive, it provides
a good introduction to horses
for young children, who may
otherwise be overwhelmed by
the size of a larger breed.

SPECIAL SIZE

The size of the Falabella is achieved by matching the smallest horses together as breeding pairs. This approach can result in a weak breed and care is taken to ensure that it remains sound. Now that the breed is well established, breeders try to mate unrelated Falabellas when breeding.

Legs may be weak and joints too close together

FALABELLA FACTS

• Miniature horses were first recorded in ancient China from 206 B.C.

• Newborn Falabellas are tiny, standing about 5 hh, and weighing around 7 kg (15 lb).

• The smallest example bred by Julio Falabella was a mare barely 4 hh and weighing just over 12 kg (26 lb).

• Falabellas can pull 20 times their own weight.

SOUTH AMERICA

Buenos Aires

PLACE OF DEVELOPMENT

In 1860, an Irishman called Newton attempted to perfect the shape of two miniature South American horses. This was later achieved by his grandson, Julio Cesar Falabella, at the family ranch close to Buenos Aires in South America.

COLOURS AND PATTERNS

The value of a Falabella often depends on its colour. As there is a wide range of colours, this has helped to increase the appeal of the horse. Both solid and part colours are accepted, but today, the spotted appaloosa pattern is particularly popular.

Brown coat

Bay coat

ICELANDIC HORSE

IN SPITE OF ITS SMALL SIZE, this animal is described as a horse rather than a pony. Originating from Norway, the Icelandic Horse has not been crossed with any other breed for more than 1,000 years and looks much like it did in the days of the Vikings. These historic horses are still used in Iceland for transport, farm work, and sport.

Neck is covered by a long mane

BARREN LANDSCAPE
The Icelandic Horse still roams across Iceland's barren landscape. It is a hardy breed, able to survive outdoors in the bitter cold of the northern winter.

Head is large and heavy compared to the body

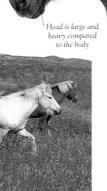

GREENLAND SEA

ICELAND

ICELANDIC SETTLERS
Horses were taken to Iceland between 935 B.C. and A.D. 860. A hundred years later, the Icelandic parliament made it illegal to import other breeds so as to keep the Icelandic Horse pure.

ICELANDIC FACTS

• Norsemen made their horses fight each other for sport.

• The Icelandic Horse can be bred in up to 15 different colours.

• These horses have taken part in races in Iceland since 1874.

Chestnut coat

Stout body and a short, strong back help the horse to carry heavy loads.

NORSE SETTLERS
The ancestors of the Icelandic Horse were brought from Norway in Norse long boats.

NORWEGIAN FJORD INFLUENCE

Together with the Tarpan, this Scandinavian pony formed the basis of the Icelandic Horse. It is dun in colour with a dark stripe running from its forelock to the tip of its tail.

Pony was formerly called the Westland

STABLE HORSE
The surefooted hooves and short, sturdy legs of the Icelandic Horse help it cover rough ground.

13

LIGHT HORSES

INTRODUCTION TO LIGHT HORSES

THE LEAN AND athletic light horse is fast and comfortable to ride. This is because of the shape of its body, with sloping shoulders and a back ideally suited to carrying a saddle. Once popular as a cavalry mount or for pulling coaches, today's light horses are used mostly for pleasure. Many modern breeds have been developed for this purpose.

Deep, compact body shape

COLORADO RANGER

COAT PATTERNS
Light horses come in a variety of colours and patterns – more so than ponies or heavy horses. The Colorado Ranger is a spotted breed. Its pattern is purely decorative and did not develop as camouflage.

LIGHT HORSE FACTS

• Light horses are famously hardy. In 1935, a group of Akhal Teke horses survived a ride of 966 km (699 miles) across the desert with little water.

• The vast herds of North American horses stemmed from 11 stallions and five mares brought over by Spanish conquistadors.

Trotting races are usually run over 1.6 km (1 mile).

MISSOURI FOX TROTTER
Light horses are fast and preferred for racing competitions. The Fox Trotter can reach speeds of 65 km/h (40 mph) while trotting in harness racing.

CATTLE HORSES

The cowboy and his horse have long been synonymous with the North American West. The speed and agility of light horses made them well suited to rounding up sheep and cattle. Their endurance meant that they could cope with long trail rides.

Palomino has a golden coat with a white mane and tail

Western bridle with curbed bit is of Spanish origin

Chaps protect the cowboy's legs from thorns.

SHAGYA ARAB

Some light horses were developed at breeding centres. The Shagya Arab comes from this stud farm at Babolna, Hungary. Early on, an Arab stallion called Shagya was involved in the breeding, giving the horses their name.

BARB

THE ANCESTORS OF this ancient horse were living in North Africa as far back as the last Ice Age. The Barb was taken to Europe by the Moors in the 7th century. Some remained when the Moors left in the early 700s and played a vital role in the development of today's breeds

HEAD DETAIL
The wide muzzle is nearly as broad as the forehead. The narrow skull is similar to the early primitive types such as Przewalski's Horse.

Head is long and nose can be curved

Curved neck is covered by long flowing mane

Shoulders are flat and upright

Deep girth and short, strong back give the breed its stamina

BARB FACTS

• The Barb was used in battle for centuries and is still ridden by Berber tribes of North Africa.

• Traditionally, Barbs are bay, dark bay, or black in colour. Grey was introduced after crossings with Arabs.

• More than a dozen of today's breeds have Barb blood in their ancestries.

MASTER OF THE DESERT
The Barb is renowned for its endurance and copes well with heat and drought. It is not a race-horse, but is fast over short distances. The Barb has Arab blood, and although there are similarities, the Barb has a heavier build.

15

COUNTRY OF ORIGIN
The Barb originally came
from the Barbary coast in
north-west Africa –
hence the name.

*Arched neck is
carried proudly*

*Strong
shoulders*

*Hooves
of tough
blue horn*

FRIESIAN
Evidence of the Barb's stamina and good
character can be found in its relative, the
Dutch Friesian. The black colour and stylish
movement of this breed made it
a popular choice for pulling
hearses in Europe during
the 19th century.

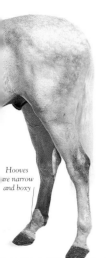

*Hooves
are narrow
and boxy*

*Short, thick
neck and
powerful
shoulders*

*Body is compact
and short with
well-sprung ribs*

LUSITANO
The Portuguese Lusitano was developed as a
cavalry and coach horse during the 1500s. It
inherited its agility from the Barb and still puts
this to good use in the bull-ring.

THOROUGHBRED

THE FASTEST HORSE in the world is the Thoroughbred and it is unlikely that a faster breed will ever be produced. This horse was developed in England during the 17th and 18th centuries especially for the sport of horse racing. Today, the Thoroughbred is at the centre of a huge international industry and is bred in over 50 countries. It is also a major influence on many other competition breeds.

STUD FARMING
The first Thoroughbreds were produced when British running horses owned by the royal family were crossed with stallions from Turkey and Arabia. Thoroughbred stud farms have been around for over 200 years, and some stallions are worth a small fortune.

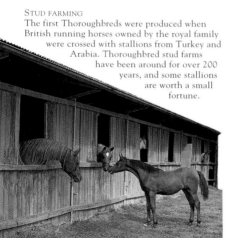

Powerful hindquarters

Long hind legs

Hard feet

QUICK COMPETITOR
Thoroughbreds start to race when only two years old, and most retire after about two years. They compete on flat ground or over fences, and can reach a speed of 70 km/h (43 mph). The first modern racecourse was set up in the 17th century near the English village of Newmarket.

Long, sloping shoulders help its easy galloping movement

UNIVERSAL APPEAL
All modern Thoroughbreds are descended from three stallions living in the mid-1700s. But it is only in the last 100 years that the breed has established its world wide appeal.

Deep chest gives good lung capacity

Coat has short hairs

Large joints

16

DUTCH WARMBLOOD

This breed of sports horse was developed in the Netherlands as recently as the 1960s. It is partly derived from the Thoroughbred, and careful breeding has made it a horse of the highest quality. Many are used for dressage.

Good muscle tone

PINTO AND PALOMINO

SOME HORSES are recognized as a breed because of their colouring. This is the case of the Pinto and Palomino which are strictly colour types and not true breeds. The Palomino has a distinctive golden colouring, while the two-coloured coat of the Pinto is associated with many other horse and pony breeds. Both horses are much in demand for western trail rides.

RIDER AND PINTO

FAVOURITE MOUNT
The Pinto's camouflage coat made it a favourite mount of the Native Americans.

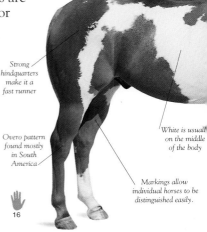

PALOMINO FACTS
• The Palomino is descended from the Spanish horses brought to the U.S.A. by settlers in the 1500s.
• The name Palomino originates from Juan de Palomino, the Spanish Don, who was given a horse of this colour.
• In Spain, the colour palomino is sometimes called Ysabella after a queen who liked it.

Strong hindquarters make it a fast runner

Overo pattern found mostly in South America

White is usual on the middle of the body

Markings allow individual horses to be distinguished easily.

16

PALOMINO COLOURING

The correct colouring is vital for a Palomino to be registered with the Palomino Horse Association. Its coat is the gold of a newly minted gold coin, and can be only three shades lighter or darker. Mane and tail must be white.

Silvery white mane

Body shape influenced by Spanish ancestry

16

Thoroughbred influence is visible in the shape of the head

PINTO COLOURING

The Pinto is also known as the paint horse. It has two types of colouring. This type, an Overo, has a coloured coat broken by white markings. The other, a Tobiano, has a white coat broken with coloured markings. No two Pintos have the same pattern.

PALOMINO FEATURES

The tail of a Palomino must be white and full. There should be no evidence of a dorsal stripe running down the back. White markings, which are often seen on the legs, must not extend above the knees, or hocks.

Full-length silvery white tail

ARAB

FIERY AND COURAGEOUS, the Arab is not only the purest of today's light horses, but it is also the oldest, having been bred for thousands of years. It has influenced most other horse breeds, especially the Thoroughbred.

Small ears are sometimes turned inwards

ELEGANT ARAB

The Arab has an elegant appearance, with a short head and a round face. Between the eyes is a shield-shaped bulge called the *jibbah*. The skin around the muzzle is particularly soft. The large nostrils help the horse to breathe easily when it is running fast.

Curved neck allows the head to turn freely

Tendons are clearly defined

15

BEDOUINS AND THEIR HORSES

Bedouin Arabs have always been closely associated with this "desert horse", which they tamed and introduced into Europe during the 7th century.

BORN IN A LEGEND
Bedouin legend traces the
Arab back to a stallion
called Hoshaba. He was
mated with a mare called
Baz, who was said to
have been captured
by Bax, the great-
great-grandson of
Noah. Notes on
breeding and
feeding these
horses can be found
in the Koran.

COSSACK
RIDER

*Tail is set high
and arches up
behind the body*

*Back is short
and slightly
curved*

*Short powerful legs
and sound hooves*

ARAB FACTS

• Napoleon rode his
grey Arab Marengo in
his final battle at
Waterloo in 1815.

• In the desert, these
horses will eat locusts,
meat, and dried dates.

• During the Crimean
War of 1851-4, one
Arab horse raced 150
km (93 miles) with no
ill effects, but the rider
died from exhaustion.

• The anatomy of the
Arab is unique, as it
has fewer bones than
other horses.

A GOOD RUNNER
In spite of its short legs, the Arab can run
for a long time. In the 1800s, it was not
unknown for desert races to last for three
days. The Arab's stamina has made it a
popular choice for the growing sport of
endurance riding, an all-day race covering
about 42 km (26 miles).

ARAB WITH
SADDLE

QUARTER HORSE

THE FIRST ALL-AMERICAN horse, the Quarter Horse is not named for its well-muscled quarters. Instead, it got its name by racing over quarter-mile (400 m) distances, often down the main street of a town. Developed by the early New World settlers, it is still used on farms.

QUARTER HORSE FACTS
• The founder of the breed was an English Thoroughbred, kept in Virginia, U.S.A. between 1756-80.
• Quarter Horses still race in quarter-mile events, such as the All-American Futurity.

COLOUR VARIATION
The colour of the Quarter Horse is influenced by its Spanish and Barb ancestors. They can be bred in any solid colour, but most are chestnut. The horse below is a bay.

Joints always move forwards, never sideways

Heavily muscled thighs

Underside of horse is longer than the back

Short bones below knee

STRONG QUARTERS
Its powerful, massive quarters help the horse to sprint almost immediately from standing and increase its speed quickly.

14

WORKING HORSE

Roping cattle, whether on the range or competing in a rodeo, is dangerous and requires a sturdy mount. Quarter Horses are often used, since they are steady and work well under pressure. They are very agile horses and possess an almost instinctive ability to follow the twists and turns of a particular cow in a herd. This enables a rider to sit securely while concentrating on roping the target animal.

The shape of the back helps to hold the saddle firmly in place.

Short, wide head

Small muzzle and shallow mouth

Wide jawbones do not restrict breathing.

Bones above front feet are sloped

MAIN FEATURES

The early Quarter Horses were part Thoroughbred and part Spanish. This produced a chunky, muscular look. Later, more Thoroughbred blood was used to make the breed faster and has given today's Quarter Horse a leaner appearance.

BUCKING BRONCO

A brave rodeo rider tries to hang on to an unbroken horse for as long as possible.

APPALOOSA

ONCE ALMOST EXTINCT, the American Appaloosa is
now one of the most numerous horses in the world.
It is distinguished by its spotted markings, although
these also occur on other breeds. As a cattle horse, it
showed its good stamina and easy-going nature. This
has encouraged its use for racing and jumping.

HISTORY OF THE BREED
The Appaloosa is descended from spotted Spanish
horses brought to America during the 16th century.
During the 1700s, it was developed by the Nez
Percé tribe of Native Americans in north-
eastern Oregon. When their territory was
taken over by U.S. troops in 1877, the tribe
was pursued and
the breed nearly
wiped out.

*Deep body with
rounded ribs*

APPALOOSA
AND RIDER

*Blanket
instead of
saddle*

BLANKET
PATTERN

*Tail is short to prevent
it getting caught on
desert scrub*

*Black and white
vertical stripes
on hoof*

15

HEAD DETAIL

An Appaloosa's head is small and elegant. The skin on its nose, especially around the nostrils and the lips, is mottled with black and white spots. For a horse to be registered as an Appaloosa, the whites of the eyes must be visible. The registry was started in 1938 and within 50 years had over 400,000 horses.

APPALOOSA FACTS

• This horse was named after the Palouse valley in Oregon, U.S.A.

• Spotted horses were first recorded in Asia and Europe more than 20,000 years ago.

• The earliest-known spotted horses came from China.

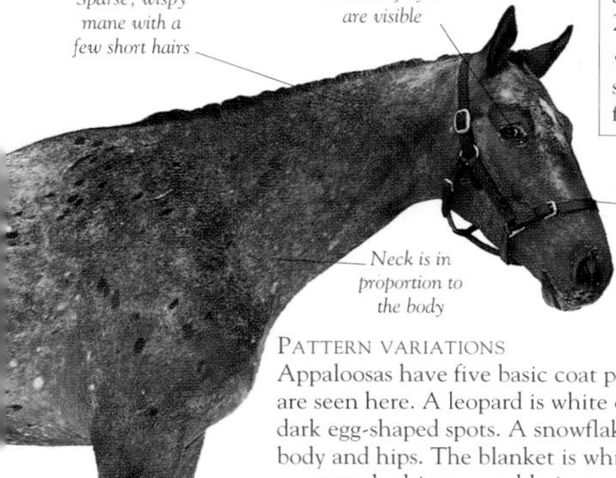

Sparse, wispy mane with a few short hairs

Whites of eyes are visible

Mottling on nose and muzzle

Neck is in proportion to the body

PATTERN VARIATIONS

Appaloosas have five basic coat patterns, three of which are seen here. A leopard is white over loins and hips, with dark egg-shaped spots. A snowflake has white spots over body and hips. The blanket is white without dark spots over the hips, a marble is mottled, and a frost has white specks on a dark background.

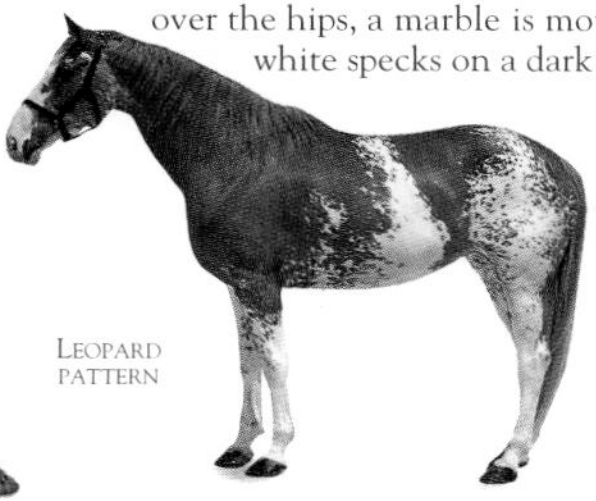

LEOPARD PATTERN

MARBLE PATTERN

ANDALUCIAN

ALSO KNOWN AS the Spanish Horse, this breed has had a great influence, particularly on the American breeds. Its origins date back to the invasion of Spain in A.D. 711 by the Berber Muslims from North Africa, whose Barb horses mixed with Spanish ponies.

Head curves outward to give a strong profile.

Strong, wide shoulders

Dapple grey coat

ANDALUCIAN FACTS

• The Andalucian has been used as the basis for royal horses of many countries including Denmark, Austria, Spain, and Britain.

• Andalucians were used in Renaissance riding schools.

• Today, the best Andalucians stem from those bred by the Carthusian monks of Jerez in Spain.

15

MAIN CHARACTERISTICS
The Andalucian's strong legs and flexible joints give it a relaxed, but purposeful way of walking. Today, most Andalucians are bay or grey in colour, but in the past, spotted and part-coloured horses existed.

Short, muscular neck is hidden by thick, wavy mane

MANE POINT
An Andalucian can be recognized by its long, dense, and often wavy mane. This helps to show the neck's highly curved profile.

SORRAIA PONY INFLUENCE
These native Spanish ponies were mixed with Barbs from North Africa to produce the Andalucian. The hardy Sorraia resists both heat and cold, and was first tamed on the Iberian Peninsula, Europe.

Body shape is similar to the ancient Tarpan pony

Decorative flowers

Special harness

SPANISH HORSE FESTIVAL
The home of the Andalucian is in southern Spain, particularly around Jerez de la Frontera, Cordoba, and Seville. Every year there is a horse fair in Jerez in which colourfully decorated horses are paraded through the streets. Andalucians are the traditional mount of the *rejoneadores* (Spanish bullfighters).

CLEVELAND BAY

DESCENDED FROM the English Yorkshire Coach Horses of the 1800s, these versatile workers pull royal carriages on state occasions. The horses are called Cleveland Bays because they originally came from Cleveland on the north-eastern coast of England. They are characterized by a distinctive bay-coloured coat with a black mane and tail.

Curved and graceful neck

Muscular neck and sloping shoulders provide power

ROYAL CARRIAGE HORSES
The Cleveland Bays used in England to pull the royal carriages are kept in the Royal Mews near Buckingham Palace in London. At one time, the Duke of Edinburgh raced a team of part Cleveland Bays in driving competitions.

16

No feathering on the feet

TRADING PLACES
The Cleveland Bay is developed from a mix of English horses, and Andalucians and Barbs brought on trading ships from Spain and North Africa to Cleveland during the 1600s. It later became known as the most powerful coach horse in Europe.

BAVARIAN WARMBLOOD

In the late 1700s, Cleveland Bays helped the development of the Bavarian Warmblood, giving it strength and stamina. This German breed is kept as a competition and carriage horse.

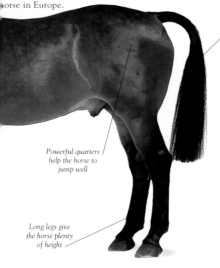

Tail is usually black, but grey hairs are a sign of purity

Powerful quarters help the horse to jump well

Long legs give the horse plenty of height

CLEVELAND BAY FACTS

• Cleveland Bays used to be called Chapmen Horses after travelling salesmen (chapmen) who used these horses to pull their carts.

• In 1962, Queen Elizabeth II bought and bred one of the last four stallions to save the breed from extinction.

• Cleveland Bays have been used as plough and draft horses on farms, as pack horses, and for carrying coal.

TRAKEHNER

ORIGINALLY DEVELOPED to take knights into battle, this horse has a long and colourful history. By the 16th century, the Trakehner was being refined into an elegant coach horse. Its bold and fearless nature made it useful for the cavalry. It is now highly valued in international sporting competitions.

Ears emphasize alert nature

Long elegant neck

Face shows horse's similarity to Thoroughbred

COMPETITION FAVOURITE
The Trakehner acquired its athletic and agile physique from earlier crossings with Thoroughbreds and Arabs. In the 1936 Berlin Olympics, the German team won every medal while riding Trakehners. Today, these horses have made a name for themselves in cross-country, jumping, and dressage events.

DRESSAGE COMPETITION

Well-balanced body moves very freely

Strong legs and joints

16

ELK-HORN BRAND

SPECIAL BRAND MARK

The Trakehner is also called the East European because of its origins in East Prussia, now part of Poland. The horses are given an elk-horn brand mark on their rear. This shape is also seen on the bridle

Powerful quarters help jumping

TEUTONIC KNIGHTS
This ancient order of knights set up the first Trakehner studs in the 1200s to supply horses for the Crusades.

THE IDEAL HORSE

Today, many consider the Trakehner as being near to the ideal riding or competition horse, with good conformation and a temperament to match. It is highly courageous, and careful breeding has ensured that it has great stamina and endurance.

TRAKEHNER FACTS

• The name of the breed comes from the site of the stud at Trakehnen, East Prussia.

• In 1945, over 1,000 Trakehners were walked 1,450 km (900 miles) to western Germany to stop them being captured by the advancing Russians.

LIPIZZANER

THESE BEAUTIFUL horses are usually associated with the famous Spanish Riding School in Vienna – so called because it has always used Spanish horses. The Lipizzaner has been developed as a classical riding horse from five stallions brought from Spain during the 16th century by Archduke Charles II, ruler of the Austro-Hungarian Empire.

Powerful hindquarters are good for rearing and jumping

Compact and muscular body with a deep chest

Strong bones and hard hooves

LIPIZZANER AND RIDER
At the Spanish Riding School it takes four to six years to train a Lipizzaner and more than twice as long to train a rider. The horses are also used for general riding, in harness, and as elegant side-saddle mounts.

AUSTRIAN STUD
The Lipizzaners at the Spanish Riding School are bred at Piber, near Graz, Austria. Eight to ten horses are selected each year.

LIPIZZANER FACTS
• There are about 3,500 Lipizzaner horses in the world.

• The breed is named after the original stud at Lipizza in Slovenia, then part of Austria.

• The horses are a select breed and all are descended from one of five stallions.

Shoulders are well suited to harness riding

Ram-like profile of the Andalucian is still evident.

COLOUR CHANGES
Adult Lipizzaners bred at Piber should be all white, but foals are dark brown or black at birth. The horses grow lighter as they mature between the ages of seven and ten. Colour variations at other studs are quite common.

White mare and dark brown foal

Short, powerful legs

16

AUSTRALIAN STOCK HORSE

TOUGH AND VERSATILE, the Stock Horse was bred to work under the harsh conditions of the Australian outback. Similar horses have been kept on cattle stations there for nearly 200 years, yet even today the Australian Stock Horse is not considered a standardized breed.

Head is heavy and chunky compared to a Thoroughbred's

Most Stock Horses are bay, but other colours are seen occasionally

Sloping shoulders are a sign of a good riding horse.

Short bones above the front hooves

STOCK HORSE FACTS

• The most famous Stock Horse is a World Event Champion called Regal Realm.

• Stock Horses make up the largest single group of horses in Australia.

• Over 12,000 Walers, sent to fight in World War I, were destroyed after the war ended. Australia's strict quarantine laws prevented their return.

RECENT BREED

After World War I, there were few horses left in Australia to work on the farms. Some of these horses were crossed with Thoroughbreds and Arabs, giving rise to the Stock Horse. It is still not accepted as a standard breed because of this mixture.

AUSTRALIA

New South Wales

SOUTH PACIFIC OCEAN

COUNTRY OF ORIGIN
Ancestors of the
Australian Stock Horse
were nicknamed Walers
after the south-eastern
state of New South Wales
where they worked.

CHARGE OF THE AUSTRALIAN LIGHT HORSES
During World War I, the British General, Allenby,
used Walers in his campaign against the Turks in
Palestine with great success. A troop of these horses
covered 274 km (170 miles) in four days, while
temperatures reached 37.8°C (100°F).

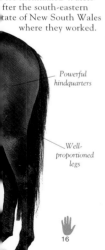

*Powerful
hindquarters*

*Well-
proportioned
legs*

16

*This Australian Stock
Horse shows Arab
influence*

OUTBACK WORK
Rounding up stray
cattle and sheep on
the vast stations of
Australia calls for a
breed with stamina
and endurance. The
first horses brought to
Australia came from
South Africa and then
from Europe. These
were superb riding
horses that could stand
up to the heat.

MORGAN AND DUTCH WARMBLOOD

THESE TWO RECENT breeds were developed specially as leisure horses. The ancestry of the Morgan can be traced back to about 1790, while the Warmblood goes back to the early 1900s. Since then, both these horses have performed well in sports competitions.

MORGAN STATUE
The Morgan is muc[h] revered in the U.S.[.] This statue is in the Kentucky Horse Pa[rk]

Fine muzzle, with small, firm lips and large nostrils

15

Colours are either bay, brown, black, or chestnut

Wide, deep chest

Long, flowing tail should reach the ground

Slender legs and well-formed joints and bones

FIRST MORGAN
The first Morgan stallion was born in about 1790 at West Springfield, Massachussetts, U.S.A. In local contests, whether pulling logs or racing, the horse beat all challengers.

DRESSAGE RIDER ON DUTCH WARMBLOOD

MORGAN FACTS

- The breed was named after its owner, Justin Morgan. Figure, the first stallion, lived for at least 28 years.
- These horses are very versatile and are used for driving, jumping, and dressage.
- Both the American Saddlebred and the Tennessee Walking horses were influenced by the Morgan.

DRESSAGE CHAMPION
The ancestors of the Dutch Warmbloods were carriage horses and this training has helped the Warmbloods to become excellent at dressage. They have also excelled at show-jumping championships.

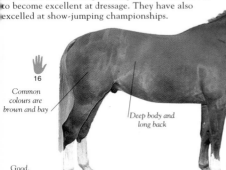

16

Common colours are brown and bay

Deep body and long back

Good, sound hooves

Well-rounded hooves

Head shape is similar to a Thoroughbred's

DUTCH WARMBLOOD
This horse is a mix of the Dutch Groningen and Gelderlander. The Warmblood was bred specifically to take part in competitions. Famous horses include Dutch Courage and Milton.

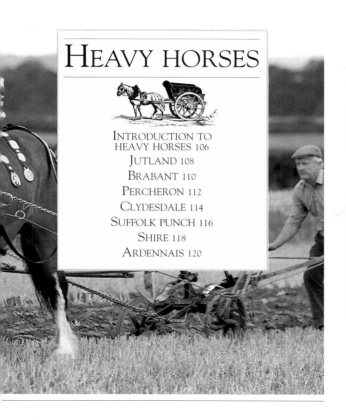

HEAVY HORSES

INTRODUCTION TO HEAVY HORSES

THE SHEER SIZE and power of the heavy horses makes them instantly recognizable. They include the largest and tallest horses ever bred. Heavy horses have a wide body and a broad back. The shoulders are upright, allowing them to be fitted with a collar, while the chest is broad and powerful.

Many heavy horses have feathering on their feet.

THE WORKING HORSES
Before mechanization became widespread, heavy horses were very much part of everyday life. Draught, or pulling, horses were harnessed to all kinds of vehicles, from wagons like the one shown here to the first buses and trams. Horses also provided muscle power in factories.

ITALIAN HEAVY HORSE

Most heavy horses were developed to be strong and to move at a steady pace. The Italian Heavy Horse was mixed with French and English breeds, and is used for light draught work in northern and central Italy.

Body of draught horse is compact and muscular

HEAVY HORSE FACTS

• The measurement "horsepower", or "h.p.", stems from the strength of heavy horses.

• Hauling matches between heavy horses were once very popular.

• The oldest heavy horse was a 62-year-old British barge horse.

FORESTRY WORK

Heavy horses are still used in forests around the world for hauling timber. Forestry work is performed better by heavy horses than vehicles, as horses cause less damage to the ground and do not need wide tracks to get into the forest.

PLOUGH HORSES

Horses have been used for ploughing the land since about A.D. 500, when the Chinese invented a special padded collar for this purpose. This made the heavy horse important to countries which relied on farming for much of their economy.

JUTLAND

CARRYING HEAVILY ARMOURED knights into battle was
all part of a day's work for the Jutland in medieval
times. On more peaceful occasions, this Danish breed
was employed on farms, ploughing fields and hauling
heavy loads over rough tracks. However,
increased mechanization means
that today Jutlands are rarely
seen working the land.

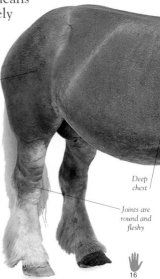

*Solid, heavy
hindquarters*

*Deep
chest*

*Joints are
round and
fleshy*

16

STILL IN HARNESS
The Jutland is ideally suited to
pulling heavy loads. Although no
longer common on farms, some are
still used to pull brewers' dray carts
through the streets of Denmark.

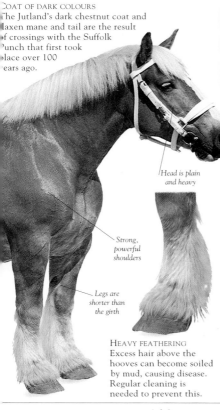

COAT OF DARK COLOURS
The Jutland's dark chestnut coat and
flaxen mane and tail are the result
of crossings with the Suffolk
Punch that first took
place over 100
years ago.

*Head is plain
and heavy*

*Strong,
powerful
shoulders*

*Legs are
shorter than
the girth*

HEAVY FEATHERING
Excess hair above the
hooves can become soiled
by mud, causing disease.
Regular cleaning is
needed to prevent this.

NORTH
SEA

Jutland
Peninsula

D...

COUNTRY OF ORIGIN
These heavy horses
are named after
Denmark's Jutland
Peninsula, where
they were first bred
over 1,000 years ago.
They have been
carefully developed
there ever since.

JUTLAND FACTS

• Viking invaders
brought the forerunners
of the Jutland to
Britain during the 900s.

• Modern Jutlands can
be traced to a British
Suffolk Punch taken to
Denmark in 1860.

• A few Jutlands have
coats coloured black,
bay, or roan.

• Though undesirable,
the heavy feathering
on the leg is an easy way to
tell the Jutland from
the Suffolk Punch.

BRABANT

THE HEAVIEST OF the heavy horses, the Brabant is also known as the Belgian Draught. This gentle giant was bred in Europe, but has gained huge popularity in the U.S.A. since it was first exported there in the 19th century. Brabants have also played a major part in the development of other heavy breeds, such as the English Suffolk Punch.

DIFFERENT TYPES
By the 1870s, there were three groups of Brabants: the *Colosses de la Mahaique* is the most powerful, the *Gris du Hainaut* has a distinctive red roan colouring, and the *Gros de la Dendre* is smaller and lighter than the others.

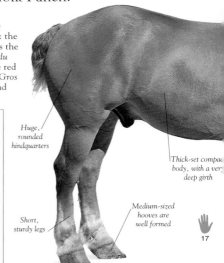

Huge, rounded hindquarters

Thick-set compac body, with a ver deep girth

Short, sturdy legs

Medium-sized hooves are well formed

BRABANT FACTS
• The world's heaviest horse was a Brabant. In 1937, Brooklyn Supreme, an American stallion, weighed in at 1,451 kg (3,200 lb).

• The Brabant is also called the *race de trait Belge* by the Belgians.

• A heavily pregnant Brabant mare was measured as having a 3.65-m (12-ft) girth.

17

STRONG AND STURDY

An exceedingly strong horse, the Brabant has a tremendously robust, yet short, back and loins. It has huge muscles, important for a draught horse since it spends most of its working life in harness. These characteristics have been carefully maintained by selective breeding.

COUNTRY OF ORIGIN
The Brabant was named after the plains area of Flanders in Belgium where it was developed. Many are now bred in the U.S.A.

Long, thick mane

Broad chest and short neck

Head is small compared to other heavy horses

Heavy feathering on lower leg

WORKING THE LAND
The Brabant was once the most famous heavy horse in Europe. During medieval times, it became known as the Flanders Horse and was much in demand as a plough horse. Suited to the variable Belgian climate and working the rich, heavy soil, this colossus was also used to pull farm wagons or dray carts in towns.

PERCHERON

ONE OF THE LARGEST and most elegant of the heavy horses is the French Percheron. It has been used in battle, on farms, as a coach horse, and, in spite of its size, has even been ridden for pleasure. Its strength and willing nature has led to many being exported to work all over the world.

Arched neck is covered by a thick mane

Fine head shape with square, straight profile

Flat nose with broad, open nostrils

Shoulders are unusually long for a heavy horse

Broad, very deep-chested body

Medium-sized hooves of hard blue horn

PERCHERON FACTS

• The world's biggest horse was an American Percheron, Dr. Le Gear, who was 21 hh and weighed 1,372 kg (3,024 lb) in 1908.

• A lighter version of the Percheron was used to haul horse-drawn Paris buses in the late 19th century.

• Percherons can pull loads of more than 1,000 kg (2,205 lb).

STRENGTH AND BEAUTY
The Percheron's refined shape comes from its crossings with Barb and Arab horses, brought to Europe from North Africa by Moorish invaders in A.D. 300. Later, Belgian horses helped to give the breed its strength.

Coat is usually chestnut, bay, or brown-bay

NORMAN COB
This breed is a lightweight draught horse. As its name suggests, it was bred in Normandy like the Percheron. At one time, the Cob was a cavalry horse.

COUNTRY OF ORIGIN
The Percheron is named after the area of La Perche in Normandy, one of the great horse-breeding centres of France.

The tail is docked to prevent reins from catching underneath.

Short, square, powerful body

Lack of feathering on the hooves is unusual for a draught horse

17

BRETON
Since medieval times, the Breton has been bred in north-western France, and its influences include both the Percheron and Ardennais. The Breton is used on farms, especially in the vineyards of the Midi region of France. There were once several types of Breton, but only two survive today.

CLYDESDALE

POWERFUL HORSES did most of the ploughing and heavy work on farms before the days of the steam engine. The Clydesdale was specially bred for this purpose and was exported from Britain to countries all around the world. It is regarded as the strongest of the heavy horses.

Long, muscular hindquarters

Head profile is straight and elegant

17

Hooves covered by heavy, silky feathering

GOOD MOVER
At one time the Clydesdale was seen as a type of Shire Horse. Although not as big, the Clydesdale shares the Shire's lively, stylish way of moving.

BREED FOUNDER
The Clydesdale was developed in the 18th century by the sixth Duke of Hamilton and another breeder, John Paterson. Together, they imported Flemish horses to increase the size and power of the local draught breeds. Later, Shire mares were also involved.

SIXTH DUKE OF HAMILTON

COUNTRY OF ORIGIN
The natural home of the Clydesdale is the Clyde Valley in Lanarkshire, Scotland. Although no longer at work on farms there, some Clydesdales still work in forests in Canada and the Russian Federation.

The rider's uniform is embroidered with gold thread.

Silver drums weigh 68 kg (150 lb) each

The rider steers by reins connected to boots and waist.

SOUNDS OF WAR
This drum horse is a 15-year-old blue roan Clydesdale. The beating of drums once inspired soldiers as they went into battle, but today the role of the drum horse is ceremonial. These two silver drums were presented to the Household Cavalry of Great Britain by King William IV in 1830.

CLYDESDALE FACTS

• The heaviest and tallest Clydesdale ever recorded weighed 1,270 kg (2,800 lb) and was 20 hh.

• In Michigan, U.S.A., one horse pulled a load of nearly 50 tonnes (tons) over a distance of 402 m (1,320 ft).

• In the days before mechanization, wheat farmers in Canada used teams of about seven horses to pull three-furrowed ploughs.

SUFFOLK PUNCH

THE TERM "PUNCH" is an old English name for a horse
with a barrel-shaped body and short legs. The Suffolk
Punch is the oldest of Britain's heavy horses. It was
developed in the eastern county of Suffolk during the
1700s. Today, every one of these horses can trace its
ancestry back to the first Suffolk, foaled
in 1768. The colour of the breed is
traditionally described "chestnut",
without the use of the first "t".

*Suffolks are bred in
seven shades; this
example is red.*

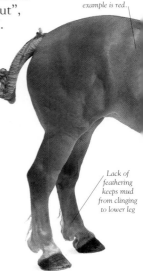

*Lack of
feathering
keeps mud
from clinging
to lower leg*

WORKING HORSES
The Suffolk Punch was developed as a
farm horse, well suited to working the
heavy clay soils of eastern England. In
spite of its bulk, it can walk a furrow just
23 cm (9 in) wide. The horses are
economical to keep and have long,
productive lives, with some continuing
to work into their twenties.

HINDQUARTERS

The immense strength of the Suffolk is partly due to its short legs and wide body. When the horse is working, its tail is often plaited up and braided in this way to keep it clear of any machinery.

Hindquarters have a great deal of power

Legs are short and muscular

This mane is plaited, ready for a show.

The powerful neck is deep and muscular.

Small ears for a heavy horse

GOOD NATURED

The modern Suffolk Punch is a big and impressive horse, with a docile and obliging nature.

Low shoulders aid the horse's pulling power

Feet are small compared to other heavy horses

JUTLAND

The modern Jutland is descended from a Suffolk Punch exported to Denmark in 1860. This Danish breed is still kept as a working horse and retains characteristics of its English relative, such as its very rounded quarters.

Heavy feathering on hooves

16

SHIRE

THE LARGEST OF ALL modern horse breeds, the Shire, is descended from the English Great Horses which were used in medieval times to carry heavily armoured knights into battle. The name "Shire" comes from the Midland shire counties of England, from where its ancestors originated.

HEAD DETAIL
The shoulders of the Shire are wide and deep. The neck is quite long for a draught horse, and slightly arched. A broad forehead, separates the large, docile eyes that give the Shire its "gentle giant" look.

Nose is slightly curved

Back is short and strong

Deep, wide, shoulders help carry a heavy harness collar.

Broad feet covered with a heavy feathering of straight hair

Dog gives an idea of Shire's size

SHIRE FACTS
• In the 1500s, the Shire was influenced by Flanders horses brought to drain the swampy English fenland.

• In 1924, a pair showed a pulling power of 50 tonnes (tons).

• Young Shires are able to work by the time they are three.

17

CART HORSES

Until the mid-1880s, the Shire was known as the English Cart Horse. Its power made it much in demand for pulling carts and working the land. Most Shires can pull loads of up to five tonnes (tons) without difficulty. Today, they can still be seen in English cities, working as draught horses for breweries. In the country, Shires appear at agricultural shows in ploughing competitions.

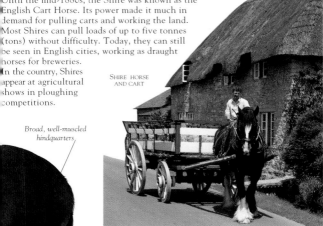

SHIRE HORSE
AND CART

Broad, well-muscled hindquarters

QUICK DEVELOPERS

A Shire has to be at least 16.2 hands high to be registered. It takes around six years for a Shire to grow to its maximum size, with stallions tending to be taller than mares. One Shire, foaled in 1846, grew to more than 21.2 hh by the time it was four and weighed almost 1,524 kg (3,360 lb).

SHIRE
MARE

SHIRE
FOAL

ARDENNAIS

THIS BREED IS regarded as the founder of the European draught horses. It also called the Ardennes, after the area between France and Belgium where its ancestors lived over 2,000 years ago. One of the oldest heavy breeds, the Ardennais has put its tremendous strength to use on both the farm and the battlefield.

Thick hair on mane

Squared off, snub nose

Heavy, muscular neck is set back into the shoulders

Dense feathering above small but powerful feet

ARDENNAIS FACTS

• Julius Caesar wrote about this horse in his accounts of the Roman conquest of northern France in 51 B.C.

• An artillery horse, it is a veteran of both the French Revolution and World War I.

• The two main types are the heavyweight Ardennais du Nord and the powerful Auxois.

BODY CHARACTERISTICS
The Ardennais has a low, flat forehead that gives it a straight profile. The ears are pricked in an alert manner and the eye sockets are prominent. The wide frame and short legs give an impression of compact strength and power.

WILLING WORKERS
The Ardennais are
gentle horses and are
managed easily. They
are still hard at work on
farms in the Ardennes,
where the harsh winters
have made them tough.
Their ancestors were used
by Napoleon's army to
carry supplies.

*Compact and stocky
body shape, with a short
back and quarters*

*Limbs like tree
trunks – thick,
short, and
strong*

16

BOULONNAIS

Like the Ardennais, the
Boulonnais is also descended
from the ancient Forest Horse
and developed in north-western
France. However, its Arab blood
has given the Boulonnais an
elegant apperance, described
as looking like polished
marble. Most are grey,
but others are bay
or chestnut.

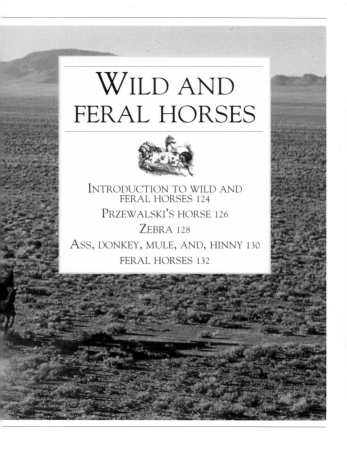

WILD AND
FERAL HORSES

INTRODUCTION TO WILD AND FERAL HORSES

FOUR DIFFERENT GROUPS of horses live in the wild: the true wild horses, zebras, asses, and feral (semi-wild) horses. All these species are grazing animals that live in herds. Sadly, though domestic horses have thrived, hunting and the destruction of their habitat have made wild horses increasingly scarce.

DÜLMEN PONY
Some ponies, like the European Dülmen, have roamed in a semi-wild state for centuries. Members of this breed have lived at Mierfelder Bruch in Westphalia, Germany since 1316. Although Dülmens resemble the British New Forest Pony, there is no link between the two breeds.

ZEBRAS
All three types of zebra live in Africa. They are easily recognized by their black and white stripes developed to deter biting insects.

Animals can go 2–3 days without water

Kulans can run at speeds up to 65 km/h (40 mph)

KULAN ASSES

Wild asses live in Africa and Asia. They prefer dry, stony habitats, where they feed on grass and shrubs. Kulans are a sub-species of onager and live in small numbers in Turkmenistan, east of the Caspian Sea.

WILD HORSE FACTS

• The onager, an ass found in Iran, can jump distances of 2 m (7 ft) or more.

• Not all zebras have stripes; some are pure black. Although rare, these live alongside their striped cousins.

• Wild horses usually spend 60–80 per cent of their time looking for food.

FERAL HORSES

In some places, domestic horses that escaped into the wild have formed feral herds. These animals are rounded up occasionally to check their health.

PRZEWALSKI'S HORSE

THIS ASIAN WILD horse was discovered in 1881 by a Russian colonel who gave the breed its name. It is an important link between the early types of wild horse and today's modern breeds.

RUSSIAN EXPLORER
Colonel N. M. Przewalski (1839-88) was a Russian soldier and explorer. By the time he made his discovery the horse was already in decline; it was extinct in the wild by 1969.

Sparse, short mane grows upright and is always partly black

Short forelock does not reach eyes

13

Dark, zebra-like markings on lower leg

Coloured speckles on muzzle and around eyes

PRZEWALSKI FACTS
• Przewalski foals are a shade of yellowish brown at birth, but are dun-coloured by the time they are adults.

• A frozen carcass 15,000 years old has been found in the northern part of the Russian Federation.

• A herd is led by the most dominant stallion, who is at least 10 years old.

CAPTIVE SURVIVORS
In 1900, Przewalski's Horses were first kept at the Askania-Nova Zoo, in the Ukraine – where the largest group lives today. In 1959, a breeding programme was started with the goal of re-establishing these horses in the wild. Today, there are more than 600 Prezwalski's horses worldwide.

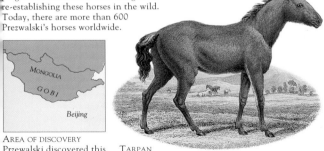

AREA OF DISCOVERY
Przewalski discovered this horse in the area of the Tachin Schah (the "Mountains of the Yellow Horses") south of the Gobi Desert in Mongolia.

TARPAN
This illustration shows a Tarpan, another Asian wild horse. Although extinct in the wild by 1879, some were kept and crossbred by Polish farmers. Recently, horses with the greatest likeness to their ancestors have helped recreate semi-wild herds.

ZEBRA

THE STRIPED PATTERN of the zebra makes it instantly recognizable. All three types of zebra live in Africa, but in different areas. Grevy's zebras can be found in the far north, the Plains zebras roam the grasslands to the east, and the Mountain zebras inhabit the uplands of the south.

GREVY'S ZEBRA
This is the largest zebra, standing 1.6 m (5 ft) tall at the shoulder. It is an endangered species – only about 7,000 remain.

Striped coat helps individual zebras blend together in a herd

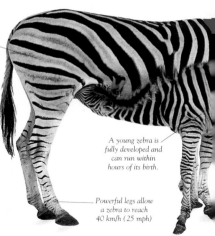

ZEBRA FACTS

• Zebras have good hearing, but they also rely on nearby animals – ostriches for sight and wildebeest for smell – to help warn them of approaching danger.

• Zebras defend themselves from predators such as lions by lashing out with their feet.

• Mountain zebras are very rare and may soon be extinct.

A young zebra is fully developed and can run within hours of its birth.

Powerful legs allow a zebra to reach 40 km/h (25 mph)

PLAINS ZEBRA

These are the most common zebras, and herds can still be seen in most African wildlife reserves. Zebras look after each other and if one member of the group goes missing, the others will search for it.

Mane stands up on back of neck

TAME ZEBRAS

A few zebras have been trained to pull carriages. This 19th-century scene shows a team of four zebras pulling a trader's vehicle, but these examples were usually gimmicks performed by publicity-conscious companies. In rare cases, zebras have been broken and ridden.

Mare and foal stay together for about five months

QUAGGA

A close relative of the zebra, the quagga lived in southern Africa. During the 1840s, these animals were hunted heavily for their meat and hides. The last survivor died in Amsterdam Zoo in 1883.

ASS, DONKEY, MULE, AND HINNY

PAIRINGS OF HORSES and wild asses have been carried out for centuries to produce working animals that are strong, yet more sure-footed than the horse. The donkey is the domesticated form of the African wild ass. A mule has a donkey father and a horse mother. A hinny has a horse father and donkey mother.

Shaggy coat

Light-coloured underside

WORKING DONKEYS
Donkeys are very strong and have been used for pulling carts in Ireland for centuries. To help them cope with the colder northern climate, these donkeys have grown thick coats.

Short brown mane

Light-coloured legs blend into the background

AFRICAN WILD ASS
The ass is the ancestor of the donkey. These asses live in herds in hot, dry regions of northern Africa.

EUROPEAN DONKEY AND CART

130

DOMESTIC DONKEYS
Many donkeys are kept as pets. They are social animals and should not be kept on their own.

Large ears

Muscular neck and heavy head

Strong, sturdy legs

Mule's stubbornness stems from its wariness of people

Hooves can become overgrown if the donkey is kept on grass.

MULE
Mules were first bred in the Middle East about 4,000 years ago. They have strong herd instincts and so work better in packs than by themselves. These groups are called mule trains.

Mane is closer in shape to a donkey's than a horse's

HINNY
Hinnies live for up to 40 years. Although they are usually sterile, on occasion they have been known to produce foals.

Colour can vary

DONKEY FACTS
• Donkeys bred in the Poitou region of France and Spain are among the largest in the world at 142 cm (56 in).
• The largest donkey ever recorded lived in Glasgow, Scotland in 1902, and was 213 cm (84 in) high.
• Miniature donkeys less than 86 cm (34 in) tall live on the Mediterranean islands of Sardinia and Sicily.

FERAL HORSES

DOMESTIC ANIMALS that have returned to the wild are described as feral. There are many horses around the world that have either escaped from their owners or have been abandoned. If they remain uncontrolled, feral horses can cause great damage through over-grazing and trampling on crops.

CHRISTOPHER COLUMBUS
The early American feral horses were descendants of Spanish horses taken to the New World by Columbus in 1493.

CAMARGUES
These white horses live in the coastal marshes of the Rhône delta, southern France, where they survive on a meagre, salty diet. They are ridden by French *gardians* (cowboys).

FERAL FACTS

• There were an estimated five million feral horses in the U.S.A. in the late 16th century.

• Small, dun-coloured feral horses living in Colombia are possibly descendants of horses brought by the Spanish conquistadors.

• Camargues are sometimes called "the horses of the sea".

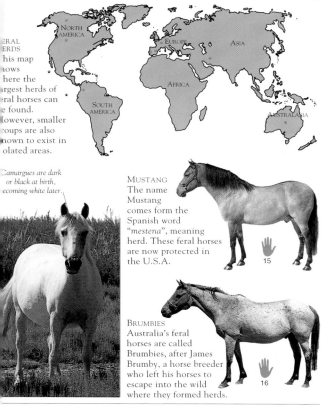

This map
shows
where the
largest herds of
feral horses can
be found.
However, smaller
groups are also
known to exist in
isolated areas.

*Camargues are dark
or black at birth,
becoming white later.*

MUSTANG
The name
Mustang
comes form the
Spanish word
"*mestena*", meaning
herd. These feral horses
are now protected in
the U.S.A.

15

BRUMBIES
Australia's feral
horses are called
Brumbies, after James
Brumby, a horse breeder
who left his horses to
escape into the wild
where they formed herds.

16

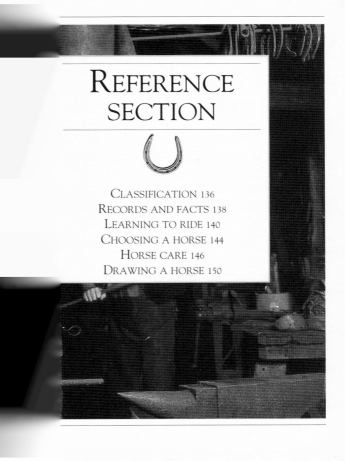

REFERENCE SECTION

HORSE CLASSIFICATION

WITHIN THE GROUP of animals known as mammals horses form part of a smaller group, the *Perissodactyla* or odd-toed mammals. Members of this group include rhinoceroses, with three toes on each limb, as well as single-hooved horses. Within this category, zebras, asses, and horses make up a small family called *Equidae*. Each species can breed with other members of the family and their offspring are called hybrids.

MULE

PART OF THE FAMILY
Although part of the horse family *Equidae*, the mule is classified as a hybrid. In most cases, hybrids are sterile. Ponies are grouped with domestic horses as they can breed with horses and produce fertile offspring.

HYBRIDS
These are offspring which have parents from two different species. Some crosses are deliberate and aim to combine qualities of both parents. Zebroids, for example, may be more suitable for working in the dry, hot African climate than horses.

MALE DONKEY	+	FEMALE HORSE	=	MULE
MALE HORSE	+	FEMALE DONKEY	=	HINNY
ZEBRA	+	HORSE	=	ZEBROID
ZEBRA	+	DONKEY	=	ZEDONK

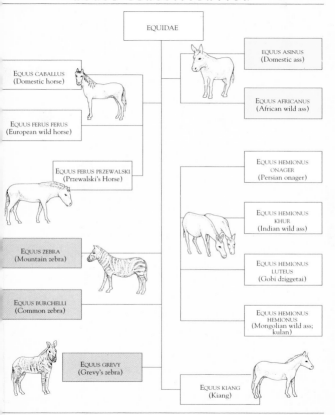

EQUIDAE

EQUUS CABALLUS
(Domestic horse)

EQUUS FERUS FERUS
(European wild horse)

EQUUS FERUS PRZEWALSKI
(Przewalski's Horse)

EQUUS ZEBRA
(Mountain zebra)

EQUUS BURCHELLI
(Common zebra)

EQUUS GREVY
(Grevy's zebra)

EQUUS ASINUS
(Domestic ass)

EQUUS AFRICANUS
(African wild ass)

EQUUS HEMIONUS
ONAGER
(Persian onager)

EQUUS HEMIONUS
KHUR
(Indian wild ass)

EQUUS HEMIONUS
LUTEUS
(Gobi dziggetai)

EQUUS HEMIONUS
HEMIONUS
(Mongolian wild ass;
kulan)

EQUUS KIANG
(Kiang)

RECORDS AND FACTS

THE SHEER DIVERSITY of horse types and breeds spread around the world has led to a number of quite amazing facts and figures. Although some are natural phenomena, many are connected with the horse's association with people, a relationship that goes back over 6,000 years.

- The tallest known horse was an English Shire called Mammoth, which stood at 21.2 hands high.

- The U.S. Pony Express ran from Missouri to California, a distance of 3,164 km (1,966 miles). This was covered by 400 ponies in a relay over 10 days.

- When spoken to, horses can distinguish particular words rather than simple tones.

- Shetland pit ponies worked underground for around 20 years.

- The oldest known Thoroughbred was a chestnut gelding called Tango Duke. It was born in 1935 in Victoria, Australia and lived for 42 years.

- The game of polo was invented by the Chinese over 2,500 years ago and was played by both men and women.

- The smallest and lightest horse in the world was reckoned to be Little Pumpkin, a miniature horse foaled in the U.S.A. in 1973. When two years old, it was 3.5 hands high and weighed just over 9 kg (20 lb).

- The heaviest weight ever pulled by two horses was recorded in 1893, when two Clydesdales pulled a load weighing 131 tonnes (tons). But recent estimates put the load at about 50 tonnes (tons).

- The most recently discovered breed was the Caspian pony, found in Iran in 1965.

- In 1277, a *destrier*, or trained battle charger, cost roughly the equivalent of a modern limousine. Less powerful horses were only a third as much.

• Horses can breed throughout their lives. The oldest horse ever to give birth was a 42-year-old Australian brood mare.

• The longest mane belonged to a horse from California, U.S.A. called Maud. It grew to a length of 5.5 m (18 ft).

• Today there are over 100 different horse breeds: 60 light horses, 12 heavy horses, and 34 ponies.

• The longest tail, measuring 6.7 m (22 ft), was grown by an American Palomino called Chinook.

• The top-earning movie horse was Tony the Wonder Horse. With cowboy film star Tom Mix (1880-1940), Tony earned around $8 million dollars in almost 300 films until injury ended his career in 1932.

• Zebras have stripes to deter biting insects such as the tsetse-fly, which can spread various diseases.

• Horses were first used for public transport in Britain in 1564.

• The first recorded race with mounted horses was at the Greek Olympiad in 624 B.C.

• Horses were first shod by either the Romans or the Celts.

• In England, people drive cars on the left. This custom stems from coaching days, when drivers drove on the left to prevent their whip (which was held in the right hand) becoming entangled in hedgerows bordering the side of the road.

• Horses have two blind spots. One is directly behind them and the other is right in front of the end of their nose.

• The last horse-drawn passenger train ran over the Fintona branch line in Northern Ireland, which closed in 1957.

• Rodeos began in the 19th century as informal contests between American cowboys. The first world cup rodeo contest was held in 1982, in Melbourne and Sydney, Australia.

• Genghis Khan operated the Yam – mounted messengers who crossed the Mongol Empire, covering 242 km (150 miles) a day.

• Millions of acres of U.S. farmland were harvested with huge machines drawn by teams of up to 24 horses.

• In 1286 B.C. at the battle of Kadesh, in present day Syria, the Hittites used 3,500 horse-drawn chariots in their defeat of Rameses I of Egypt.

LEARNING TO RIDE

RIDING CAN BE ENJOYED at any level, from a gentle hack in the country to taking part in national competitions. The rider progresses through different stages and learns how to control the horse while developing balance and rhythm. Having a good instructor and learning the correct methods from the start is the best way to begin.

RIDING SCHOOL
The ideal place to learn to ride is at a registered riding school with qualified instructors who can help riders correct their mistakes quickly.

EQUIPMENT
Riders should dress for safety and comfort. Some special items may be needed for riding in the dark.
1 Warm jumper for cold weather. 2 Tweed hacking jacket for everyday wear. 3 Hard hat covered with silk.
4 Stretch jodhpurs for freedom of movement.
5 Jodhpur boots.
6 Long leather, or rubber boots. 7 Gloves.
8 Stirrup torch.
9 Fluorescent belt for night riding. 10 Cross-country whip.

MOUNTING UP

1 Stand on left of horse facing tail. Hold reins in left hand placed in front of saddle and turn stirrup iron outwards.

2 Put left foot into stirrup iron and face horse's side. Hold bottom of mane with right hand and push off ground with right leg.

3 Swing right leg over horse's back, turn body to face forward and lower body into saddle. Place right foot in stirrup iron.

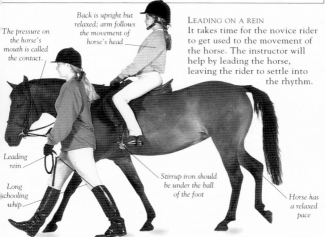

Back is upright but relaxed; arm follows the movement of horse's head

The pressure on the horse's mouth is called the contact.

LEADING ON A REIN
It takes time for the novice rider to get used to the movement of the horse. The instructor will help by leading the horse, leaving the rider to settle into the rhythm.

Leading rein

Long schooling whip

Stirrup iron should be under the ball of the foot

Horse has a relaxed pace

The different paces

A horse moves its legs in a different sequence for each change of pace, from a trot to a canter to a gallop. Riders must learn to keep their body movements in time with the rhythm of the horse.

TROT

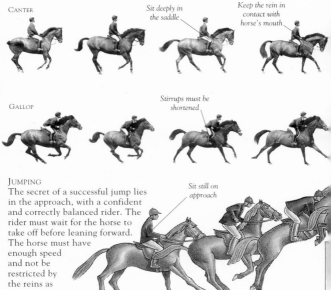

CANTER

Sit deeply in the saddle

Keep the rein in contact with horse's mouth

GALLOP

Stirrups must be shortened

JUMPING

The secret of a successful jump lies in the approach, with a confident and correctly balanced rider. The rider must wait for the horse to take off before leaning forward. The horse must have enough speed and not be restricted by the reins as it jumps.

Sit still on approach

Keep hands still

TROT
The trot is quite a bumpy movement. Riders learn to let the horse throw them up in the saddle and land back lightly.

Press with the inside of the legs to help keep horse moving

CANTER
The rider's back is relaxed to move in harmony with the rocking motion of the horse. The hands follow the movement of the horse's head.

Lean forward from the hips

Hands stay on either side of neck

GALLOP
The rider sits forward and rises slightly out of the saddle to take the weight off the horse's back, allowing it to go faster.

Keep head up and eyes straight ahead

Ensure lower legs are held straight under the body

CHOOSING A HORSE

OWNING A HORSE requires considerable commitment, both in time and money. The horse must above all be suitable for the purpose in mind. It is better to buy privately rather than at an auction as this allows a closer inspection. The horse should be ridden and then checked closely by a vet before a final decision is made.

FURTHER EXPENSES
Apart from the cost of the horse, there will be stabling, food, and veterinary bills. You will also need to buy equipment, such as saddlery and clothing.

9-10 YEARS 15 YEARS

19-20 YEARS 20-25 YEARS

TEETH
The front teeth can be used to tell the age of a horse. As the horse ages, the slope of the teeth increases and they become discoloured.

Saddle must fit properly

Riding clothing can be expensive.

Horses need to be shod every four to six weeks.

WHAT TO LOOK FOR

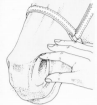

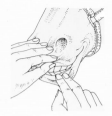

NOSE

The nostrils should have large air passages and be thin and flexible. When the horse is at rest, they should be almost closed. If not, there could be a breathing problem.

EYES

Poor eyesight can cause a horse to shy away from things. The eyes should be clear and free from tears, the pupils black, and the eyelids thin and smooth.

TEETH

The front teeth should be level; otherwise, the horse will be unable to graze properly. Check for damage in the mouth caused by an unsuitable bit or sharp teeth.

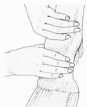

HOOFS

The wall of the hoof should be smooth, not cracked or brittle. The hoof must be symmetrical with the shoes worn evenly – an uneven fit might indicate a defect.

LEGS

The tendons should be hard and sinewy and not soft and puffy. Soreness or swelling is a sign of a recent or previous injury. Trotting on a leading rein may show lameness.

COAT

Check for swellings and blemishes on the back, often made by a badly fitting saddle. The coat should be clean and shiny. A dull, scaly coat is the result of parasites.

HORSE CARE

A STABLED HORSE needs constant grooming. This not only improves its looks, but also keeps the horse healthy and feeling good. Horses living in fields develop oils, giving their coat a natural gloss that can be removed by continual washing.

STABLE RUBBER

DANDY BRUSH

BODY BRUSH

WATER BRUSH

SWEAT SCRAPER

HOOF OIL AND BRUSH

HOOF PICK

METAL CURRY COMB

PLASTIC CURRY COM[B]

MANE COMB

SPONGE

WASH AND BRUSH UP
Stabled horses should be groomed thoroughly at least once a day. Grooming includes a number of tasks and special tools are needed to do each job properly.

CLEANING HOOVES
Clean the horse's hooves out every day using a hoof pick. This removes any matter which could collect moisture and allow germs to infect the hoof.

SPONGING THE FACE
Using water and a special sponge, clean the nose, eyes, and lips separately. Wash the sponge out thoroughly afterwards.

COMBING THE TAIL
After untangling any knots, brush out the tail carefully so as not to pull out any hairs. A damp brush will flatten the shor[t] hairs at the top.

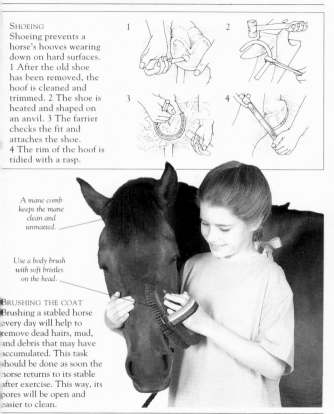

SHOEING

Shoeing prevents a horse's hooves wearing down on hard surfaces. 1 After the old shoe has been removed, the hoof is cleaned and trimmed. 2 The shoe is heated and shaped on an anvil. 3 The farrier checks the fit and attaches the shoe. 4 The rim of the hoof is tidied with a rasp.

A mane comb keeps the mane clean and unmatted.

Use a body brush with soft bristles on the head.

BRUSHING THE COAT

Brushing a stabled horse every day will help to remove dead hairs, mud, and debris that may have accumulated. This task should be done as soon as the horse returns to its stable after exercise. This way, its pores will be open and easier to clean.

Finishing touches

Extra attention can be given to a horse if it is to be prepared for a show. After washing, the mane and tail can be plaited. This also helps the mane fall in the right way later. Oiling the hooves makes them look smart. Bandages are used to protect the horse's legs when it is being transported and give it extra support and warmth during exercise. The coat can be made to look more attractive by careful clipping and combing.

1 PLAITING A MANE
Dampen the mane and plait it in sections, starting at the top.

2 ROLLING UP
Pass a plaiting needle through the bottom of each plait and roll it up.

3 FINISHING OFF
Push needle through knot and wind thread round to hold it in place.

PLAITING A TAIL
Start the plait at the top and gradually work down, with the ends forming a long pigtail. Secure this with an elastic band and turn it up into a loop which is then stitched to form a thick double plait. Ensure it is not too tight.

Plait whole tail to the bottom of the dock

Continue plait to the end of the tail and sew back in a loop

Unplaited hair hangs loose

CLIPPING AND COMBING

The type of clip a horse receives depends on the sort of work it will do and how much it sweats. For a show, patterns may be made on a horse's rear by combing through a template in a different direction to the rest of the coat.

OILING HOOF

Oil must not go on the hair above the hoof.

Hoof brush

HOOF CARE

Applying hoof oil to the hoof's wall prevents it losing moisture and becoming dry and brittle, as well as smartening its appearance. As the hoof grows, it will need trimming to prevent the wall from becoming too long and splitting.

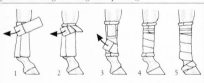

BANDAGING LEGS

Leg bandages are wrapped over a soft lint padding. 1 Start from the top. 2 Wrap bandage in same direction as padding. 3 Finish off midway up the pastern. 4 Exercise bandage helps support the tendons. 5 Stable bandage prevents damage.

CHECKER-BOARD COMB

CHASER CLIP

HUNTER CLIP

SHARK'S TEETH COMB

DRAWING A HORSE

SKETCHING OR painting a horse is a good way to become familiar with the shape of its body. Practise from pictures before drawing a real horse, which will move about. First, draw a quick outline and fill in the details later. Experiment with different techniques, including charcoal and pencil. When confident, try using some coloured inks.

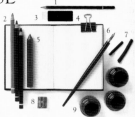

ARTIST'S TOOLS
You will need a set of basic artist's tools. 1 Drawing pencil. 2 Selection of coloured pencils. 3 Eraser. 4 Clipboard and paper. 5 Thick pencil. 6 Ink pen. 7 Willow charcoal. 8 Pencil sharpener. 9 Coloured inks.

DRAWING THE HEAD
The horse's face not only reveals its breed, but can be surprisingly expressive and full of character. Try to capture some of this in your sketch. Much of the head is made up of small circular lines. Rehearse a line before actually drawing it. Carefully mark where short or long lines will finish and use these marks as guides.

1 Begin by drawing the outline of the nose. These vertical lines provide a good reference point for the other features.

2 As you build up the structure of the head draw small, faint, circular lines to give overall shape to the cheeks and eye sockets.

THE WHOLE HORSE

Try to capture the whole of the horse at a glance. Draw it quickly to suggest fluidity and agility. At first, sketch very loosely and lightly, using a pencil to get the shape of each part of the body.

1 With eyes half closed, sketch an outline of the body and neck. Concentrate on the shape of the muscles, especially around the quarters, which will convey a sense of power.

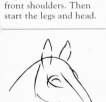

2 Make sure the horse's hindquarters are slightly higher than the front shoulders. Then start the legs and head.

3 Look at the shapes created by the spaces between the body and legs, to help you find the correct proportions.

4 Finally, shade in the details of the body. Shadows emphasize the muscles and give the horse a solid look.

3 Complete the outline with rounded strokes to form the mane, mouth, cheek, and ears. Keep the lines light at this stage.

4 Now draw in the eyes, fetlock, and nostrils. These major features start to suggest the horse's character and expression.

5 Using the guide lines, add shading to give the head three-dimensional form. Rub out any unwanted guide lines.

Resources

United Kingdom

Association of British Riding Schools
Mrs J. Packer
Old Brewery Yard
Penzance
Cornwall
TR18 2SL

British Equestrian Association
Wothersome Grange
Branham
Nr Wetherby
West Yorkshire
LST 6LY

British Field Sports Society
59 Kennington Road
London
SE1 7P2

British Horse Society, British Show Jumping Association, and the Endurance Riding Group
British Equestrian Centre
Stoneleigh
Kenilworth
Warwickshire
CV8 2LR

British Show Pony Society
Mrs P. J. Hall
124 Green End Road
Baltry
Huntingdon
Cambridgeshire
P17 5XA

Horse and Hound Magazine
Kings Reach Tower
Stamford Street
London
SE1 9LS

Horse and Rider
296 Ewel Road
Surbiton
Surrey
KT6 7AQ

Hunters Improvement and National Light Horse Society
96 High Street
Edenbridge
Kent T98 5AR

International League for the Protection of Horses
Anne Colvin House
Snetterton
Norwich
NR16 2LR

Master of Foxhounds Association
Parsoles Cottages
Bagendon
Cirencester
Gloucestershire
GL7 7DU

National Pony Society
Willingdon House
102 High Street
Alton
Hampshire
GU34 1EN

Pacemaker and Thoroughbred Breeder
38-42 Hampton Road
Teddington
Middlesex
TW11 0JE

Ponies Association UK
Chesham House
56 Green End Road
Baltry
Huntingdon
Cambridgeshire
PE17 5UY

Riding for the Disabled Association
National Agricultural Centre
Stoneleigh
Kenilworth
Warwickshire
CV8 2LR

Australia

Australian Endurance Riding Association
MS 16
Maleny
Queensland 4552

Australian Pony Stud Book Society
GPO Box 4317
Sydney
New South Wales 2001

Australian Riding Pony Association
Seymour Road
Nar Nar Goon
Victoria

Australian Stock Horse Association
PO Box 288
Scone
New South Wales 2337

South Australia Horse Society and **South Australia Horse Driving Society**
Fisher Road
Hahndorf
South Australia 5245

Western Australia Horsemen's Association
50 Bombard St,
Mount Pleasant
Western Australia 6153

NEW ZEALAND

Canterbury Horse & Pony Breeders Society
c/- Killinchy
RD Leeston

New Zealand Driving Society
c/- Mrs I Cochran
Root Street
Fielding

New Zealand Pony Clubs Association (Inc.)
Private Bag 502
Putaruru

New Zealand Riding Pony Society (Inc.)
Swanmore
Marsh Road
Halswal
Christchurch 3

Welsh Pony and Cob Society of NZ (Inc.)
c/- Collier
RD 5
Taihape

DENMARK

Danish Riding Federation
Idraettens Hus.
2600 - Glostrup

ICELAND

Icelandic Pony Horsebreeding Division Agricultural Society of Iceland
Baendahollinni
Box 390,
Reykjavik

IRELAND

Field and Country Sports Association of Ireland
M. C. A. Jackson
Ferndale
Kilpedder
Gracestones
County Wicklow

Irish Horse Board
Irish Farm Centre
Dublin 12

Irish Horse Trials Society
Miss M. Spiers
12 Bridge Street
Hillyleagh
County Down
BT30 9QM

SOUTH AFRICA

Endurance Riding Association of South Africa
P.O. Box 30
Halfway House 1685

Polocross Association of South Africa
P.O. Box 314
Eastcourt 3310

South African National Equestrian Federation
P.O. Box 52365
Saxonwold 2132

JAPAN

Nihon Bajutsu Renmei
Kanda Surugadai 1 – 2
Chiyoda – Ku
Tokyo

Zenkoku Jouba Club Shinkou Kyoukai
Kami – Ohga 2 – 1 – 1
Setagaya – Ku
Tokyo

Glossary

ACTION
The way a horse moves its body.

AGED
A horse of seven or more years old.

AGEING
Estimating the age of a horse from its teeth.

AIDS
Signals made by the rider to communicate with the horse.

BLEMISH
Permanent mark caused by injury or disease.

BLINKERS
Flaps on the bridle to ensure the horse can only see straight ahead.

BLOOD STOCK
A racing Thoroughbred.

BLUE FEET
Blue-black colouring of the horn on the feet of some breeds.

BONE
Circumference around the leg beneath the knee or hock, which influences the ability of the horse to carry weight. Used in the term "big boned".

BREAKING-IN
The initial training of a horse, to allow it to be ridden or harnessed.

BREED
A group bred selectively for particular features over many generations, and recognized on the basis of these characteristics.

BRIDLE
Equipment used to control a horse's head.

BROOD MARE
A mare used for breeding.

BRUSHING
A conformational fault, with the hoof or shoe striking the opposite fetlock.

BUCK
Leaping into the air: the back is kept arched, and the horse lands on its stiff forelegs.

CARRIAGE HORSE
A light horse used for pulling carriages.

CHESTNUT
The horny, oval-shaped area on the inside of the forelegs and hocks.

COLD-BLOODED
Horses with ancestors originating from the cold climates of north-western Europe.

COLLAR
Part of a harness worn by a heavy horse for pulling loads.

COLT
Ungelded male horse under four years old.

CONFORMATION
The shape and proportions of the horse's body.

CROSSBREEDING
The mating of two horses of different breeds or types.

DAM
Mother horse.

DORSAL STRIPE
Dark hairs extending down the back towards the tail.

EQUIDAE
Family of mammals comprising all horses, ponies, asses, and zebras.

ERGOT
Horny growth located on the back of the fetlock.

FARRIER
Someone who makes horseshoes and shoes horses.

FETLOCK
A tuft of hair that grows above a horse's hoof.

FILLY
A female horse under four years old.

FOAL
A horse under a year old.

FORELEGS
The front two legs of a horse.

FROG
The triangular-shaped pad on the bottom of the horse's foot that acts as a shock absorber.

GAIT
The way a horse moves.

GELDING
Castrated male horse.

GIRTH
Circumference of a horse's body measured from behind the withers.

HOCKS
Bones forming the knees of the rear legs.

HARNESS
Collective term for equipment used to control a draught horse.

HAUNCHES
The hips and buttocks.

HOT-BLOODED
Horses with ancestors originating from hot Middle Eastern countries.

MANE
Long hair on the back of a horse's neck.

MARTINGALE
Item of tack used to increase control of a horse's head, or to alter the pull of the reins.

MARE
A female horse more than four years old.

MULE
Offspring of a male donkey and female horse.

NEARSIDE
The left side of a horse, where it is usual to saddle-up and mount.

NUMNAH
Pad placed under the saddle to prevent chafing or rubbing.

OFFSIDE
The right side of a horse.

PEDIGREE
The ancestry of the individual horse.

POINTS
External features, responsible for the horse's conformation.

PONY
A horse not exceeding 14.2 hh.

PURE-BRED
A thoroughbred.

REINS
The strap attached to the bit.

STALLION
An ungelded male horse over four years old.

STUD
A stallion kept for breeding.

STUD BOOK
The breed society's record, featuring the pedigrees of pure-bred stock.

TACK
All saddlery, riding, and driving equipment.

TYPE
A horse that fulfils a specific function, rather than a specific breed; for example Hunter Type.

WARMBLOOD
Horses which are half- or part-bred, resulting from thoroughbred and Arab crosses with other breeds.

WITHERS
Part of the horse above the shoulders where the neck joins with the body.

Index

Acknowledgements

Dorling Kindersley would like to thank:
Hilary Bird for the index.

Special photography by:
Akhil Bakhshi; Peter Chadwick; Gordon
Clayton; Steve Gorton; Kit Houghton; Colin
Keates, Natural History Museum, London 24-
5, 77tc, 127br, 129br; Bob Langrish; Ray
Moller; Tracy Morgan; Stephen Oliver 91-2;
Tim Ridley; Karl Shone; Jerry Young.

Illustrations by:
Joanna Cameron; Tony Graham; Will Giles;
John Hutchinson; Janos Marffy; Sean Milne;
Sandra Pond; John Temerton; John
Woodcock; Debra Woodward.

Picture credits:
t=top b=bottom c=centre l=left r=right
Animal Photography/Sally-Anne Thompson
69cr, 89tr, 108cl;/R. Willbie 124bl, 132br.
Bridgeman 86bl. Bruce Coleman/Steve C.
Kaufmann 125tl;/Fritz Prenzel 76-77, 82bl;/
Jonathan Wright 122-123. Susan Daniel 73tc.
ET Archive 101cr. Mary Evans 97tr, 126tr,
129tr, 132tr. Werner Forman Archive 71cr.
Hamilton Collection, Lennoxlove House,
Haddington, Scotland 115tl. Robert Harding
13tr, 54bl, 56cl. Michael Holford 14cr & br,
15cl. Kit Houghton 48-49, 52bl, 60br, 65br,
67tl, 83tc, 94bl, 104-105, 116cl. Bob
Langrish 31cl, 35tl, 53br, 59b, 90bl, 93br, 107bl & bc,
119tr, 121tc, 124br. Peter Newark's American
Pictures 89br. Only Horses 36br. Oxford
Scientific Films/ M. Austerman 127tl.
"Complete Guide to Equitation" by Norman
Thelwell published by Methuen, London.
Zefa 99br.

Horse names and owners:
3br *Rajah*, West Midlands Mounted Police;
10-1 *Barone*, Mr Tavazzani; 21cl *Duke*, Jim
Lockwood; 22-3 *Brutt*, Robert Oliver; 34tr
Lyphento, Conkwell Stud; 40-41 *Quist and
Rajah*, West Midlands Police; 41tl *Nibble*,
Kinstroop; 50-51 *Lockinge Edward*, Abigail
Hampton; 53tr *Little Trouble*, Marvin
McCabe; 52-53 *Parlington Pepsi & Dulcie*, Mrs
Johnston; 54-5 *Little Elska*, G & H Greenfield;
55br *Blue Print*, Mervyn & Pauline Ramage;
56-7 *Warrendale Duke*, Mr Dickson; 57tr
Waverhead William, Mr & Mrs Errington; 57br
Sunbeam Superstar, David Vyse; 59t *Blyth
Jessica*, M. Houlden; 58 *Murrayton Delphimus*,
June Freeman; 61 *Bowerwwood Aquila*, Mrs
Rae Turner; 62 *Blackhill Sparkle*, Mrs Crump;
63 *Malibu Park Command Performance*, K & L
Sinclair; 64-5 *Spinway Bright Morning*, S.
Hodgkins; 65tr *Llanarth Sally*, Mr & Mrs
Bigley; 66 *Chi Chi*, Steve White; 67 *Clover*,
Kenneth Burton; 68 *Dinolino*, Josef Waldherr;
68-9 *Nomad*, Miss Helen Blair; Hopstone
Shabiz, Mrs Scott; 72-3 *Pegasus, Cleopatra and
Bernando of Kilverstone*, Lady Fisher; 75br
Ausdan Svejk, John Goddard Fenwick and Lyn
Moran; 78t *Skippers Valentine*, T J Crouch;
81br *Montemere-O-Nova*, Nan Thurman; 81tr
Sjouke, Sonia Gray; 82-3 *Ardent Lodger*, Mr &
Mrs Duffy; 83br *Restif*, Haras National De
Compiègne, France; 85 tr,br *Wychwood
Dynascha*, Mrs G. Harwood; 84tr, 84-5 Hill
Man, Boyd Cantrell; 88bl *Doc's Maharaja*,
Harold Bush; 93tr *Campanero XXIV*, Nigel
Oliver; 94-5 *Oaten Mainbrace*, Mr & Mrs
Dimmock; 95tr *Samurai*, Heiner Eppinger;
96-7 *Muschamp Mauersee*, Janet Lorch; 98-99
Saglavy Szella, J. Goddard Fenwick and Lyn
Moran; 100 *Scrulo Victory*, Mrs Waller; 102b
Shaker's Supreme, Fred & Bonnie Neuville;
103br *Tokyo Joe*, Lorna Tew; 108-9 *Jorgan
Nielsen*; 110-1 Roy Kentucky Horse Park,
USA; 113br *Tango & 112-3 Ibis*, Haras
National de San Lô, France; 114 *Blue Print*,
Mervyn & Pauline Ramage; 116-7 *Laurel
Keepsake II*, P. Adams & Sons; 117tr *Tempo*,
Jorgen Neilsen; 118-9 Jim Lockwood; 120-1
Ramses du Vallon Haras, National de Pau,
France; 121br *Urus*, Haras National de
Compiègne; 133cr *Patrick*, Kentucky Horse
Park; 133br *Pone*, Ron & Anna Baker; 146b
Ovation, Robert Oliver.

Every effort has been made to trace the
copyright holders and we apologize for any
unintentional omissions. We would be pleased to
insert the appropriate acknowledgements in any
subsequent edition of this publication.